HUMANITIES PROGRAMS TODAY

RICHARD R. ADLER

Editor

Assistant to the Executive Secretary
National Council of Teachers of English

CITATION PRESS · NEW YORK · 1970

To
Mike and Steve
and their generation

LIBRARY OF CONGRESS CATALOG CARD NUMBER: 73-135165

Standard Book Number: 590-04722-1

CONTENTS

Ninth-grade, inter-city girls; one-semester course of three consecutive daily periods; integrates history, English, art, music, dance, drama, foods, clothing, science, philosophy, and economics by studying four cultures; parental involvement encouraged.

BURNT HILLS-BALLISTON LAKE JUNIOR HIGH SCHOOL,
BURNT HILLS, N.Y.   70
Norman Ward Wilson
"An Image of Man: The Beginning, the Defects, and the Struggle to Be an Individual"; units combine music, art, literature, social studies, and philosophy under English department; team-teaming; stresses perceptual awareness; utilizes electronic environmental learning center for independent study.

THE MILNE SCHOOL, CAMPUS SCHOOL OF THE STATE UNIVERSITY OF NEW YORK, ALBANY, N.Y.   76
Roy York, Jr.
Three offerings: (1) two periods per week for seventh- and eighth-graders (2) eight or nine weeks as a unit of English 12, and (3) full-year elective instead of English 12; all use allied art approach, resource people from the University, and multi-media.

ALAMEDA HIGH SCHOOL, ALAMEDA, CALIF.   80
Mary Frances Claggett and Madge Holland
One or two semesters of elective "English by Individual Design" for juniors and seniors; discovery of self and relationships of self to society; problem-solving, inductive methods; flexible content.

CONCORD-CARLISLE HIGH SCHOOL, CONCORD, MASS.   84
Socrates A. Lagios
Academically disinterested juniors and seniors; program based on values related to the themes "The Dignity of Man" and "Who Am I?" inductive, multi-media methods.

team-teachers and guests; discussion encouraged; individual projects in art, literature, music, and drama.

RIVER DELL REGIONAL SCHOOLS, ORADELL, N.J. 115
Helen H. Winn
Anthropological and philosophical focus; required of all seniors; separate humanities department but works closely with English department; multi-media; team-teaching and guests; large and small group instruction; individual creative projects.

ANN ARBOR PIONEER HIGH SCHOOL, ANN ARBOR, MICH. 125
David E. Tabler
Interdisciplinary elective for college-bound seniors; concentrates on selected examples of intellectual and artistic expressions of Western man; lectures and small seminars but no independent work; daily double periods; special interest mini-courses offered during last three weeks.

NORTHPORT HIGH SCHOOL, NORTHPORT, N.Y. 130
Morris Saxe
Geared to students' concerns and questions; emphasizes human values and ideas; flexible, changing, open-ended content; grades and tests minimized; multi-media experiences and field trips; full-year elective for seniors; double periods; team-teaching.

OAK PARK AND RIVER FOREST HIGH SCHOOL, OAK PARK, ILL. 141
Morris S. Buske
Two-year "World Civilization" course for ninth- and tenth-graders of average ability; history, art, and music teachers; large and small group instruction; comparisons, critical analysis, research, and tolerance of differences stressed; heavy use of films and tapes.

DAVID H. HICKMAN HIGH SCHOOL, COLUMBIA, MO. 146
Conrad Stawski
Elective for seniors of average and better ability; team-

taught by English instructors; survey and analysis of art forms and exposure to art experiences; individual creative projects; guest lecturers, multi-media, and field trips.

ST. MARIA GORETTI HIGH SCHOOL, HAGERSTOWN, MD.   150
Sister Mary Sharon, SSND
Stresses experiences with and integration of the arts of Western and non-Western world, grades based on class participation—no tests; multi-media, field trips, and demonstrations; flexible content geared to seniors' backgrounds; monthly individual creative projects.

LAKEWOOD HIGH SCHOOL, LAKEWOOD, OHIO   154
William F. Hamilton
Professional and student monthly auditorium presentations of drama, music, dance, art, literature, poetry, or a combination of these arts for all juniors and seniors; pre- and post-classroom discussions; cooperation with nearby college in cultural activities.

ROBERT A. MILLIKAN HIGH SCHOOL, LONG BEACH, CALIF.   157
Neil Van Steenbergen
Full-year honors course for gifted and academically talented seniors; modified team-teaching; three 12-week units in political philosophy, the arts, the man, society, and values; seminar-discussion techniques; spring weekend retreat extends classroom exchanges and readings; one-semester non-honors course also offered.

NORTHERN VALLEY REGIONAL HIGH SCHOOL AT DEMAREST, DEMAREST, N.J.   164
Eugene E. Best
Voluntary, non-credit summer course open to all students, grades 9–12; inquiry methods; field trips and multi-media; also full-year elective for seniors; thematic structure; team-teaching and small-large group instruction; flexible scheduling.

CRISPUS ATTUCKS HIGH SCHOOL, INDIANAPOLIS, IND. 169

Judith R. Waugh

Interdisciplinary approach to history, literature, music, and art; team-taught; two semesters for academically able students; flexible syllabus; students report on outside-school cultural events and prepare original compositions.

FRANKLIN DELANO ROOSEVELT HIGH SCHOOL, HYDE PARK, N.Y. 172

Dean S. Northrop

Structured around units on music, painting and sculpture, dance, opera, poetry, drama, and architecture; selected seniors experiment with and participate in all art forms; modified team-teaching; field trips and multi-media; individual creative projects replace final exam.

MARBLEHEAD HIGH SCHOOL, MARBLEHEAD, MASS. 176

Dorothy Miles

One-semester "Man in Conflict" course for non-academic seniors; chronological and ideological study of the forces that have impelled Americans into armed combat; read historical novels, poems, and essays about the various wars; multi-media and field trips.

DOBBS FERRY HIGH SCHOOL, DOBBS FERRY, N.Y. 180

Nancy Moore

Required two-semester courses for ninth and tenth grades; both interdisciplinary, team-taught, value-oriented, flexible grouping, and multi-media; separate humanities department; daily three-period time blocks; humanities 9 organized around six units on cultural past and heritage; humanities 10 has six thematic units emphasizing modern man; CCTV facilities.

PALISADES HIGH SCHOOL, KINTNERSVILLE, PA. 186

Helen G. Severs

Twelfth-year English students of all ability levels

study the literature, drama, poetry, art, architecture, and music of five thematic-cultural eras; flexible, changing approach, content, and requirements; student involvement in arts and discussions encouraged; multi-media resources.

NORTHWESTERN HIGH SCHOOL, DETROIT, MICH. 192
Eula Gayl Cutt
Four elective semesters of "Latin Heritage" to give inner-city, educationally deprived students a knowledge and appreciation of the Graeco-Roman world; under aegis of foreign language department; Latin is not taught in traditional fashion but used to strengthen English language skills; multi-media materials; some team-teaching.

THE EDUCATIONAL LABORATORY THEATRE PROJECT, NEW ORLEANS, LA. 196
Shirley Trusty
Brings living theatre and classical literature to 10–12 grade students in public and parochial schools as part of English curriculum; study packets for teachers and principals and reading copies for students usually provided prior to each of four annual presentations; workshops, actors' visits, and theatre tours.

ATLANTA PUBLIC SCHOOLS, ATLANTA, GA. 200
Lucille G. Jordan
Humanities approach to all instruction being developed and applied throughout elementary and secondary systems; extensive in-service experiences for teachers; curriculum revisions for four-quarter, 12-month program; multi-media, role-playing, discussion, field trips, and use of community resources.

FOREWORD

THIS BOOK HAS GROWN out of the professional concerns of its editor. It was conceived because humanities programs are increasing in the elementary, middle, and secondary schools, and because daily letters request "anything available" on humanities programs.

The authors who contributed did so to help others attempting to establish effective humanities programs in their schools. The editor has tread lightly on these descriptions to keep intact each program's unique personality and flavor. Each program is tailored specifically to a community, a school system, a teaching team, and to available school and community resources.

As the reader will discover, certain characteristics spark the life of each program: student engagement, de-emphasis on grades, interrelationship of disciplines, contemporary topics, independent study, exploration of media — all pursued in a relaxed classroom atmosphere.

Students and their teachers constantly evaluate and change the course of study to insure interest. What is relevant this year or semester may fade from the scene for future study. This continuous evaluation is partially responsible for the success of these programs. Perhaps it is significant that humanities programs do not remain static and consequently defy the categorization, labeling, and structuring that have solidified and regimented other disciplines.

For their professional and personal concern, I thank the authors who contributed these program descriptions. My grateful appreciation also goes to Dr. Jerry L. Walker for the introduction to this book. And to my wife, Carol, who cares, my thanks for her assistance.

Richard R. Adler

Jerry L. Walker, Professor, University of Illinois, and Program Chairman of the 1968 National Humanities Conference
An introductory summary of the objectives, investigative methods, and organizational requirements of meaningful humanities programs, which basically should be a study of man's values.

MORE THAN TWENTY YEARS AGO Leslie White wrote in his book, *The Science of Culture,* that technology has a way of creating its own culture and that as technology advances, culture changes faster and faster. He also said that in a technological culture, man has little control over its development, that culture becomes a force that perpetuates itself, more or less dragging man behind it. I think Leslie White was right, and as I try to analyze the alienation, the disjunction, and the disharmony in our country today, I feel confident that most of it has developed as a result of man's sudden awareness that the kind of life he has been living simply does not fit with today's culture. Fortunately or unfortunately, culture will not stop for us. It will continue to change, and if we would keep up, we must learn to change along with it.

Keeping up with a fast-changing culture is difficult. We are slowed down by the baggage we carry with us — our language, our values, our myths, our memories, our beliefs, and our attitudes, all of which are tied together like pieces of rag forming the tail of a kite (and anyone who has flown a kite knows that if the tail is too long and heavy, the kite will hardly lift off the ground). The youth in our culture have a couple of advantages over adults. First, they were born into a time marked by faster change and have developed a greater tolerance for it; and second, they have accumulated less baggage because they have not lived so long. However, they operate under a great disadvantage, too, because adults have given them a lot of the same baggage that they carry.

We cannot abandon the past. Even if we could, it would be a foolish thing to do. What we do need to do is to analyze very carefully what is needed to live today and what was needed to live yesterday and then get rid of what will not be needed to live tomorrow.

The school is the place where that ought to be done. No longer can the curriculum be primarily devoted to teaching about the past and what was heretofore known, believed, and valued. If the school is to prepare students to live in harmony with today's world and to develop leaders for tomorrow's world, it must be present and future orientated, drawing upon the past only as it is useful today and tomorrow. It must be devoted to developing the student's analytic and imaginative powers more than his memory. The school, not the streets, must become the forum for inquiry.

Within the school's present structure, the best place to do the job is in a humanities class, which seems to be the one place where students are not treated like walking memory banks that must be fed only facts and figures. In addition, in most humanities courses students are encouraged to feel as well as to know, and that is a great plus.

Not all existing humanities courses are good, however. Some of them are devoted to the same sterile telling and remembering characteristic of most science courses. Some of them are the same kind of chronological surveys that mark the worst college English courses, only the subject is broader. Some are restricted to students with the highest measured IQs, as if they were the only students able to profit from such study. Some are devoted to bringing students to "high culture" so that they will be able to enjoy the "better things in life." And some are devoted to refining the student's taste in an effort to make him an art critic.

Needless to say, those are not the kinds of humanities programs we need. Instead we need humanities programs that are truly devoted to what it means to be human in today's world. They must be built on the premise that meaning is not absolute, that it may change from day to day and from student to student. Analyzing, questioning, hypothesizing, and testing must be the methods of investigation. And a tentative answer, not a firm conclusion, must be the goal.

What should be the organizing thread of a humanities program? I am not sure it makes much difference whether the thread is American studies, culture epochs, great ideas, or values, as long as certain conditions are met. First, the study should begin with the present with a view to the future. Second, students should be the ones who select the topics, problems, or ideas that they are going to study. Third, the program should be open to all students, the fast as well as the slow, the bright as well as the dull, the college-bound as well as the non-college-bound; and the classes should be heterogeneously grouped. Fourth, the idea of coverage should be abandoned; a humanities program that begins with the notion that certain things must be covered is bound to fail. Fifth, grading should be abandoned in a humanities course. As long as students know their performance is to be graded, it is virtually impossible for them to avoid thinking that there are "right" answers to be learned, remembered, and fed back to the teacher. And sixth, the teacher must not think of himself as the repository of all knowledge. He must see himself as one who can involve students in an investigation by presenting them with a provocative stimulus, helping them formulate significant questions, guiding them to useful sources of information, and encouraging them to test their tentative answers.

15

Let me illustrate how such a humanities class called "American Studies" might work. I would begin by buying or acquiring from the library as many current periodicals as I could, and I would want the range of subjects and types to be as wide as possible, including such publications as weekly news magazines, women's magazines, art, dance, and theater magazines, teen-age magazines, sports magazines, men's magazines, romance magazines, and even comics. I think I might simply ask the students — individually or in groups — to investigate those magazines and answer the question, "What questions do these magazines raise in your mind about the American way of life?" If the students did not, or could not, respond to that, I would probably ask more specific questions: "What are some of the social problems dealt with in these magazines?" "What seem to be our main interests?" "What are our major political problems?" "If a stranger came to the United States, and before going out to see the country and meet people, he looked through these magazines, what would he expect to find?"

After the students had raised their own questions and answered them, or answered the questions I had asked, I would ask them to identify what they consider the most important questions and answers. Then I would encourage extensive discussion and investigation of these issues, making sure that they drew upon wide resources for justification and verification. Sometime during the course of the investigation I would ask them if they thought these same problems will exist a year hence, making sure that they address themselves to possible causes and solutions. In their attempts to answer that question, they might find it useful to look at the same periodicals of a year or two earlier to see if they could detect evidence as to whether the problem had existed then, whether it had changed, or whether we seem to have solved part of the problem. If the problem seemed to be a long-standing one, I might ask them to try to find out when and where it began and to try to figure out why we had not been able to solve it.

After all that would come the look at the future: "Will these problems remain with us?" "Why or why not?" "What will we have to do to solve them?" "Can you as an individual do anything?" "What are some of the topics and issues you would expect to find appearing in these magazines a year from now?" "Why?"

Essentially, then, that is how the course would go. Certainly there would be no shortage of things to discuss, investigate, and test. That there is so much to do might even be a problem, and in that case I would try to encourage the students to narrow their focus, to zero in on only a few aspects of American life. I would want the students to end up with some tentative hypotheses about the future of our society and their role in it, and I would urge them to test their hypotheses in as many ways as possible. There would be no tests and no grades, but students who had engaged in such a study would be better prepared to succeed as human beings in our American culture.

Humanities courses using culture epochs or great ideas as the organizing theme could follow almost the same pattern. Using the broadest definition of culture in the study of culture epochs, I would begin by leading students to an identification of our present culture — its institutions, its art, its social customs, its patterns and means of work and recreation, its religions, its human relationships, and its technology. When questions arose regarding how or why our culture is like it is, I would direct them to look at past cultures as well as other current cultures. From there I would lead them to hypothesize about the stability or the likely direction of change of various parts of the culture they had identified. The emphasis throughout would be on the role of the individual and the part he played yesterday, must play today, and will play tomorrow to achieve harmony in the existing culture.

A great ideas course could follow basically the same pattern, beginning with a wide-ranging search for the ideas that seem to have affected the way man lives today and ending with some hypotheses about the stability of those ideas and whether they are likely to change. Throughout that study I would want students to see how ideas become embodied in our customs, myths, the things we produce, and the things we value. I would want them also to investigate how ideas originate, how they become accepted, and how they are perpetuated. Such a course should generate some new ideas — new, at least, for the students — and influence their future actions.

There are many roads to Mecca, including one paved with aesthetics. This road is probably not so direct, but I think it would lead to the same kind of self-awareness, reflection, and insight as the others. In an aesthetics course, my concern would be more with students' responses than with the art that stimulated them. I would be more concerned that students be able to understand and articulate their responses than to recognize or categorize a work of art. The two, of course, are not entirely separate, but I believe that it is the response to a work of art that should be studied, not the work of art itself.

The study of art should lead to greater self-awareness and sensitivity, and I would begin by asking students to express their preferences in the various arts — dance, drama, prose, poetry, design, architecture, sculpture, music, and so on. Always they would be encouraged to bring in examples of things that turn them on and to discuss the reasons for that. If it became obvious that there were certain modes, forms, or media that some students had not experienced, I would be sure to make these available to add to their repertoire of responses. Always the primary question would be, "What does your response tell you about yourself?" Any response that was sincere and honest would be accepted, and I would strongly discourage talking about good or bad, adequate or inadequate, knowledgeable or ignorant responses. Without the teacher's complete acceptance of student responses, the students will not respond honestly. What I hope would emerge is a clear understanding on the part of each student of what he likes, why he likes it, and whether he is satisfied with his taste. That kind of self-knowledge should lead to a decision regarding whether or not change is needed, and I would settle for a decision either way, for the person who has reached such a decision is better prepared to cope with tomorrow.

My preference for unifying a humanities course is through the study of our cultural symbols and the values they imply. So far as we know, man is the only animal capable of symbol-making. It is that ability that allows him to reflect on his past, record his present, and imagine his future. The aim is control. Man can partially control what he can order, and he orders through the use of symbols. Man orders in a preferred way, and his symbols reflect that preference. Any study of man's symbols will therefore be a study of what he prefers, that is, what he values.

Whatever man invents can be viewed as a symbol: his language, his artifacts, his institutions, his forms of recreation, and his means of subsistence. As symbols they necessarily reflect values or preferences. Take language, for instance. There are some Indian tribes and South Sea islanders whose languages contain no means of expressing the past or future tense. This does not mean, as some people assume, that theirs are underdeveloped languages. It means only that these people have developed a language that expresses the way they prefer to think of time. There is no past for them, only the present. In these cultures there is little evidence of remorse or even hope. How could there be, with no past or future to contend with? One has to assume that these people have developed a language that expresses their values, and to them the present is of great value.

Take our own language, which contains several ways to signal past, present, and future. We obviously prefer to think in these terms. We believe in the continuity of time, and we value it. If we did not, we would not be so hung up on original sin. Consider also our language preference for the active voice. English teachers are constantly telling students to recast a passive construction into an active one. Certainly that is a reflection on our values. We would rather do than be done. We value the active man.

If you consider our homes as symbols, it becomes clear that we value convenience, comfort, privacy, cleanliness, easy upkeep, and moderate durability. A look at our schools shows that, among other things, we value tradition, role authority, book learning, sports, punctuality, perseverence, and neat classes of people and material. Our games reveal competing values — cooperation and competition. We urge people to work together on a team and then pit teams against one another. Our institutions such as marriage show that we value possession, responsibility, security, male authority, and contractual commitment. Take a look at our jobs, and you find we value ingenuity, speed, convenience, and coffee breaks. In whatever we arrange, we express our values.

Man not only creates things to symbolize his values, he also selects objects from the natural world and gives them symbolic value; that symbolic value is usually recorded in his language and art. Consider the statements "solid as a rock," "strong as an ox," "delicate as a rose," and "sly as a fox." Consider paintings of a sunset or sunrise, of a turbulent or calm sea, or of a pastoral scene and what they symbolize. Notice the symbolic difference between catching a trout and catching a marlin or the difference between killing a lion and killing a jackal. What values are men operating on when they select such emblems as doves, eagles, and wolverines for their crests? Much can be learned about man's values, both his hierarchy of values and conflicting values, from a study of the natural objects he bestows with symbolic value.

The study of values is the study of man. He is the only animal capable of thinking beyond his immediate drives and the present stimulus. He can consciously modify his behavior in preferred ways. He expresses these preferences through his behavior and through his symbols. To know man, to predict how he will behave, or to change his behavior, one must know what he values. Those values should be the content of a humanities course.

Here are some of the kinds of questions that might be studied in such a humanities course: "Is there a natural order in the world?" "What is to be gained from assuming a natural order?" "When did the idea first gain popularity?" "What effect has it had on man's development?" "How do modern scientists view natural order?" "Where in literature can you find acceptance of the idea of natural order?" "Where in art?" "Where would modern architects stand on the issue?" "What are some of the objects man has used to symbolize natural order?" "What symbolizes natural order to you?" "If you accept the idea of natural order, what are the implications for the way you live your life?" There are hundreds of similar questions, of course, that could be asked about the same topic, all of which would require that students draw upon their knowledge of the past and present and end up with a clearer view of their own values. Whether they change their values or not, they will at least have had to identify and consider them, and having considered them, they will be better prepared to live in a changing culture.

Throughout this introduction the terms "humanities program" and "humanities course" have been used interchangeably because in many schools one humanities course is the extent of the humanities program. That one course is usually called, variously, "American Studies," "Great Ideas," "Cultural Heritage," "Aesthetics," or even "Art Appreciation." As a beginning, one course is fine, but what is needed is much more than that. What is needed is a continuing dialogue among students, year after year beginning with the middle grades, concerned with those problems they face individually and collectively.

The curriculum of the future ought to provide as part of every school day a block of time devoted to open seminars that all students must attend. There will certainly be in the future more individualized study and more ability grouping in those subjects that can be articulated in terms of specific knowledge and skills — practices that will make it even more urgent for schools to make provision for all students to come together to discover and discuss common concerns. It is inevitable in a technological society that we will become more specialized in our functions and more isolated within our narrow range of interests, and while we may be aware of changes occurring within our own area, we may be completely out of touch with changes in other areas. Without continuing dialogue, we are apt to remain ignorant of changes that affect us and to begin to think of ourselves as so unique, specialized, and distinct from others that we could lose sight of those qualities and concerns that inextricably bind us together. The exploration of those qualities and concerns and what they mean in our presto-chango culture should really be the essential subject matter of any humanities program, whatever it is called.

What follows in this book are brief descriptions of some humanities programs and courses as they are being taught in various schools throughout the country. It is interesting to note how many of the authors indicate that the course of study is always changing. That, of course, is as it should be. Times change, students change, teachers change, and issues change. A humanities program that becomes fixed and static is apt to lose its most important characteristic — vitality.

What these descriptions can do is give some good ideas on how to begin a humanities program. Most of them provide valuable insights into the use of materials, staff, and grouping procedures. Before using any one of these program descriptions as a model, however, teachers and administrators would do well to keep these questions in mind:

1. Is this program geared more to the exploration of ideas than to the memory of facts?
2. Is this program past, present, or future oriented?
3. Will this program encourage imagination and creativity?
4. Is this a program in which all students can participate?

5. Can we provide the staff, materials, space, and time needed to make this program a success?
6. Is this a program dominated by the students and their concerns?
7. Is this a program that can turn on a turned-off generation?

If the answers to those questions are affirmative, and if the program is then put in operation, solutions to those human problems that so frequently beset today's schools may well be in the making.

Jack Strauss and Richard Dufour*
Sixth-grade course to aid transition to junior high; "Discovering Who I Am"; six-week unit with weekly themes; stresses role-playing, creativity, and principles of semantics in literature, art, and music.

Rationale — "Discovering Who I Am" is a six-week unit integrating literature, social studies, art, music, semantics, and media for the sixth grades in the Fairfield school system. It is intended to be the first of three opportunities to study the humanities. Presently Fairfield offers a senior elective, "The Humanities in Three Cities," to provide a transition from high school to college or the world. The present course is designed to provide a transition from the intermediate to the junior high school level. It is hoped that a third offering will be developed to offer a transition between the junior and senior high school.

"Discovering Who I Am" calls upon the students to use all the skills and knowledge learned in the first six years and provides them with an opportunity to probe into the problem of identity as one of the most important areas of knowledge. The course has been designed to take advantage of three factors. The fact of transition between levels of the sequence has been mentioned, but more importantly, the course is based on the findings of Piaget, who has indicated that during the age range from 12 to 15 one of the major changes in the cognitive development of students takes

---

* A fuller description of this program by Messrs. Strauss and Dufour is "Discovering Who I Am: A Humanities Course for Sixth Grade Students," *Elementary English,* January 1970, pp. 85–120.

place, and attendant findings of psychologists who have labeled this period as one of radical changes in the emotional development of students. For all of these reasons, a course in the humanities designed to share with students the ways, the means, and the values of investigating the meaning of human experience would seem to be particularly relevant.

Objectives and Approach — For this first exploration into the humanities, the central concern of both the content and method is the problem of identity. For this reason the materials and the content of the course may seem somewhat strange to those familiar with humanities courses concerned with the arts and their relation to man. It is not really a departure from the tradition of humanities courses, however; rather, it places maximum stress on the statement of the Commission on the Humanities that, "The humanities is the study of that which is most human." The authors of the present course have committed themselves to the premise that before the arts can become relevant, the student who is being exposed to them must be aware of the "I" who is doing the experiencing. Hence the structure and the content of the course place a primary stress on materials and methods of achieving a sense of identity rather than on the arts. The major objective of the course and its principal approach might well be stated as:

> Human maturation is more than a process of learning "things"; it involves the gradual creation of a "role," a unique and accustomed manner of relating to "others" — persons, things, situations — outside the self that will determine and characterize all of a person's social behavior. Part of growing up is the learning and developing of this role, not solely as a factor of social status or social identification but also as a matter of personal identity. A person's role is not only his patterned way of evaluating and behaving toward the world of others; it is also his way of evaluating and behaving toward himself. In these terms all behavior is the reflection of a role, and all social

In short, the aim of the course is to develop what Dr.
Charles Keller has called "an inner space program" for
students who will be undergoing rapid changes in their intellectual, emotional, and social relationships in the bewildering years of junior high school. Furthermore, the authors
agree with Dr. Keller that "the sciences help us to live, but
the humanities we must have if we are to live well." What
Dr. Keller has stated so succinctly, Charles Schulz has
visualized in one of his most memorable cartoons. Readers
may remember the five frames in which he has outlined the
eternal optimist, Charlie Brown, and the eternal pragmatist,
Lucy, against a starlit sky. As they sit on a grassy hilltop
looking up at the heavens Charlie says, "The stars are beautiful, aren't they? I think that there must be a tiny star out
there that is my star. And as I am alone here on earth among
millions of people, that tiny star is out there alone among
millions and millions of stars. Does that make any sense,
Lucy? Do you think it means anything?" Charlie Brown's
question is answered with brutal frankness by Lucy, "Certainly. It means you're cracking up, Charlie Brown!" It is
our feeling that too many Charlie Browns receive such
answers. It is perhaps to provide him with help and support
in discovering answers and to enable him to reply to the
question, "Who do you think you are, Charlie Brown?"
which Lucy is always throwing at him, that we have designed this course.

Knowledge Objectives:

1. To know that the humanities help us understand and
   define the many roles we play as we develop an identity.
2. To know that the thoughts and feelings that emerge as

the self relates to varying social situations have been for others and can be for us the source of all the arts.

3. To know that to create or understand the arts requires an insight into the self and an understanding of the form and the materials used by the artist.

4. To know that values grow out of and determine reactions to the experiences we have with both other people and the arts.

Affective Objectives:

1. To develop a personal definition of honesty, fair-mindedness, rules, self-acceptance, prejudice, revenge, rejection, friendship, responsibility of individuals and groups.

2. To recognize the uniqueness of each person.

3. To display a desire to identify with the real worlds and imaginations of other children and adults.

4. To develop a commitment to looking at language as a clue to misunderstanding and conflicts.

5. To recognize the role of the senses in acceptance and rejection of ideas.

Inquiry Objectives:

1. To be able to apply personal definitions to new situations.

2. To be able to consider the variety of possibilities that may be involved in arriving at the explanation of phenomena.

3. To be able to state an "educated guess" on the basis of knowledge and observations.

4. To be able to recognize what values are reflected and promoted in a work of art.

5. To be able to express ideas in original ways.

Course of Study — The course concentrates on role-playing to explore group behavior and the dilemmas of the child as he searches for his identity and his personal values. Occasions constantly arise when a child's inclination to act properly is in conflict with fear or with other positive values. Since the student must be helped to discover, not merely be told about, such characteristics as kindness, generosity, and loyalty, experiences must be provided that permit such discovery. As George Mead indicated in his article, "A Behavioristic Account of the Significant Symbol" in the *Journal of Philosophy:* "The self arises in conduct, when the individual becomes a social object in experience to himself. This takes place when the individual assumes the attitude or uses the gesture which another individual would use and responds to it himself or tends to so respond."

"Discovering Who I Am" structures its materials to present a maximum opportunity to let the student explore the self as it arises in conduct and provides him opportunities to explore and express the self in the forms of art, literature, music, and drama. The stress in all areas is on the role of values in making decisions related to identity.

A second major stress is on the role of creativity in the development of identity. The authors believe with Hughes Mearns in his book *Creative Power,* that "All God's chillun got wings" but that all too frequently they are not permitted to use them. To quote Mr. Mearns, "The creative spirit is something more than a product in print, clay, or canvas: it is dancing, rhythmic living, a laugh, a flash of the mind, strength of control, swiftness of action, an unwritten poem, a song without words; it is life adding its invisible living cells to more and abundant life." The products of the arts do not serve as objects of study for their own sake but as the means to tempt the student to consider their relevance to the problems of identity and then to fly with the wings God gave him.

Because role-playing and the arts are all involved in symbol-making and symbol-receiving, a vital adjunct to the various facets of the course is developing some of the principles of semantics. The role that language plays in human affairs is vital to a sense of the relationship of the self to the world, and the symbolic process in all the arts is basic to coping with the problems treated in the course. Hence those principles that treat the roles of symbols in thought and feeling are a unifying thread. If the course is to aid students in feeling what they know and knowing what they feel, they must be able to control the means of expressing such knowledge. Semantics would seem to offer a means of developing such insight.

The humanities, in whatever format a course is structured, is basically a course in questions. One of the simplest definitions of the self is that part of man that attempts to discover answers to the questions posed by experience. It should not be assumed that the questions posed would not be concerned with the arts. Art can and is used as the medium for creating experiences that force questions with which the emerging identity of the student must cope. However, to quote Marshal McLuhan, "the medium is the message," and the message requires understanding. Understanding requires questions about the arts, and among such questions would be: "What is meant by the arts?" "How have the arts come to be so important?" "Where do the arts come from?" "Who says the arts are important?" and "Why aren't other areas more highly ranked than the arts?"

Requirements — The content of "Discovering Who I Am" is related to six weekly themes that explore area of identity. They are drawn from three of the major elements of the humanities: literature and language, art, and music. The themes are: "I've Got a Name," "Brothers, Sisters, Mothers, Fathers, and All Those Relatives," "The Other Kids," "Sticks and Stones," "Mirrors and Doors — The Arts," and "The Inner Space Program." Each section consists of selected readings with analytical questions. The purpose of the readings and the questions is to lead students to experiences that will help them define the meaning of the word "humanities," arouse in them interest in the arts and the media, and help them see themselves as human beings in a world of human beings.

All the material is designed to be taught inductively. That is, the student is presented with a wealth of data he uses to come to some conclusion, explanation, or interpretation of the material. The student is expected to develop his own interpretations through skillful use of the inquiry methods, defined in the skill objectives. The teacher's task is to guide the student to his answers. Lesson plans have been developed to provide suggestions as to how this may be carried out.

Materials

I've Got a Name, Holt, Rinehart & Winston (basic text, teacher's guide, and record).

This series provides the teacher with student materials, suggestions for lessons, motivational and developmental strategies, and evaluation procedures. It will serve as a valuable tool for those lessons using stories from the text and will also suggest materials and strategies for role-playing and other procedures for lessons not taken from the text itself.

Who Do You Think You Are, Charlie Brown?, Charles M. Schulz, Fawcett Publications (student).

This paperback of cartoons provides a daily ritual for beginning each new lesson. The cartoon for the day serves as a point of departure for a four-step procedure followed by each student for each cartoon. He will be asked to read the assigned strip, fill in appropriate information on the bone structure, and complete a sentence and a paragraph for the notebook. Complete instructions are included in the lesson plan for the first week.

Role Playing for Social Values, Dr. Fanny and George Shaftel, Prentice-Hall (teacher).

This text will serve as a guide and a frame of reference for both theory and practice in this integral part of the unit work. Particular attention should be given to "Checklist for

Guiding Role-Playing," pages 183–188, and to the "Problem Stories," pages 203–425.

Creative Power: The Education of Youth in the Creative Arts, Hughes Mearns, Dover (teacher).

This classic in the methodology of developing the creativity inherent in *all* children will serve as both stimulus and model for the teacher who wishes to really commit her class to expression through the arts.

The World of the Arts, The Child's World Encyclopedia (teacher).

This supplement to the encyclopedia series, *The Child's World,* provides a comprehensive and readable survey of the arts with readings and exercises geared to sixth-grade students to aid them to comprehend and appreciate the goals and methods of the artist in his expression of experience. It should serve as a valuable resource to the teacher in supplementing and enriching the unit.

The Allied Arts, Missouri State Department of Education (teacher).

Although this is a guide for high school humanities courses, the introduction and background should be read as a guide for planning lessons and structuring class exercises.

Language in Thought and Action, S. I. Hayakawa, Harcourt, Brace & World (teacher).

This most popular of all the texts on semantics should be consulted by the teacher as background for the theory and strategy of the lessons on semantics and language included in the unit.

Sometimes Gentle, Elementary students from Center School, New Canaan, Connecticut (student).

This is a delightful collection of poetry and artwork by youngsters of elementary age.

Harvey R. Wall

Invitational summer program for advanced sixth-graders; "Exploration in the Arts and Sciences: An Attempt to Better Understand Man's Relationships to Himself and His Environment"; independent study, common group exposures, and field trips; modified team-teaching.

Rationale — Summer sessions have provided personnel in the Mt. Diablo Unified School District the opportunity to offer students content and methods that go beyond the conventional school year curricula. For various reasons, advanced programs have been frequently developed in mathematics and the sciences to the potential neglect of curricular changes in the humanities and social sciences for the more able students.

When planning the framework for a summer invitational program for advanced elementary level students, several basic assumptions were accepted:

1. Advanced elementary students need a continually increased awareness of their surroundings so that learnings from the environment can be initiated through stimulations from a school program.
2. One of the more satisfactory vehicles for encouraging this awareness could be found in the humanities and cultural arts.
3. As a means of furthering individuality in student thought and behavior, an independent study-seminar instructional

approach could satisfactorily relate to the characteristics of advanced students.
4. Teachers strongly committed to a liberal education and possessing a strong interest in the humanities would best stimulate student interest and awareness in their broadly defined environment.
5. Actual exposure to a sampling of tangible resources available to the student in his environment provides reinforcement for theoretical instruction in the classroom.
6. As students increase their awareness to environmental resources, family involvement in cultural expansion follows.

Objectives — Because this program was pilot in nature, selected aspects were, of necessity, trial balloons based upon the assumptions just stated. Purposes and objectives were:

1. To offer students learning outside of the conventional curriculum.
2. To increase student awareness and sensitivity to the many opportunities for ongoing self-education outside of the classroom.
3. To assist the student in gaining a broader orientation to men through his more refined expressions.
4. To expose the student to independent study and seminars at the pre-adolescent level of development.
5. To expose the student to his intellectual peers on a total classroom-program basis.
6. To examine potentialities for future summer programs and provide evidence for implications for conventional classroom curricula.

Approach — Robert Boone, principal of San Miguel School, and Miss Janice Davis, teacher in El Monte School, planned their presentations around the theme, "Explorations in the Arts and Sciences: An Attempt to Better Understand Man's Relationships to Himself and His Environment."

To realize this broad instructional goal, the two fundamental approaches of independent study and common group exposure were employed. Modified team-teaching permitted all students to experience both teachers through daily rotations of class groups. Changes within groupings occurred as well when, in the judgment of the instructors, different interest and participation patterns emerged in students.

Choices of content in the humanities were determined by a combination of teacher and student interest areas as revealed by interviews and inventory responses. Although the student inventory results influenced the content of the total group exposure somewhat, most general presentations were influenced by teacher interests and decisions. Small group and independent study content areas reflected student interests.

Students — Developmentally, terminating sixth-grade students were considered the most capable of bringing maturity to the abstract and independent nature of the program — a reasonably safe assumption for elementary school children. Because buses return students to the Fine Arts Summer School (Clayton Valley High School) well after the close of the school day, seven elementary schools in reasonable proximity to it were selected to minimize pupil distribution problems. Invitations to attend were sent to terminating sixth-grade students who had been identified and previously placed in advanced programs in Mt. Diablo, Clayton Valley, Westwood, Ayers, Ygnacio Valley, San Miguel, Walnut Acres Elementary Schools.

All seven schools were represented among the 41 enrolled students (22 boys, 19 girls).

Requirements — Each student studied an area of interest in depth and orally reported his findings. In addition, a minor topic about which the pupil knew little or nothing was chosen. Throughout the reports and concomitant questions from classmates, the prevailing concern was, "What impact has this area made upon mankind?"

Topics ranged from history, archeology, architecture, and mythology, to water purification, establishment of a radio station, and the operation and functioning of the nervous system. In some cases students conducted interviews with specialists in the field, and in one instance tape recorded the discussion for classroom presentation.

Research techniques were continually integrated into the ongoing study efforts. Instructors stressed critical thinking as the independent activities developed via questions such as: "Why?" "How do we know this?" "What evidence can you offer to support that statement?" "How valid and reliable are your sources of information?" and "What are the pros and cons?"

Course of Study — In a communication to the parents near the end of the session, the teachers briefly summarized the exposures given all pupils and their basic intent:

> We have tried to expose youngsters to many areas, in the cultural arts particularly, to which they might not be exposed in the course of their regular school experiences. It is hoped that this will be just the beginning of an interest — not the end of it. As teachers we have each tried to capitalize upon our own strengths in giving to the class an exposure they might not get from the other teacher. In some cases we both treated the same subject in a different manner.

It is, at best, difficult to itemize the topical array encompassed by so broad a curricular attempt as humanities and the cultural arts. Incidental discussions about the unique and verbalized interests of the students frequently caused the groups to depart temporarily from the intended subject area of the day. Thus, the following common learnings of the classroom scene represent teacher-organized subjects only:

Artists and their art: Discussions embraced the questions, "How did the period in which the artist lived influence his style and how did his life experiences influence his interpretation of life?" Studies of artists and their art included: Van Gogh, Rembrandt, Modigliani, Chagall, Brueghel, Da Vinci, Renoir, Picasso, the Lascaux caves, Toulouse-Lautrec, Gauguin, and the Rococo period.

Photography: Legitimacy as an art form was stressed with discussions related to the photographer's use of contrast, texture, design, color, form, human interest, and general composition as vehicles for conveying graphic intent. Some of the photographers considered were Ansel Adams, Werner Bischof, Robert Capa, Philippe Halsman, and Edward Steichen.

Architecture (buildings and landscape): An architect's integration of site requirements, function, environment, and design into a final product was studied through the specific works of men such as Frank Lloyd Wright, Yamisaki, Edward Stone, Christopher Wren, and Antonio Gaudi.

Illustrators of children's books: The unique art of literary illustration was examined through the work of Kay Nielsen (*East of the Sun and West of the Moon*), N. C. Wyeth (*Treasure Island*, et al), and Arthur Rackham (*Wind in the Willows* and *Rip Van Winkle*).

Literature: Exposures and studies ranged from Greek mythology to H. G. Wells, from *Winnie the Pooh* to Michener. More specific learnings pertained to:

Jack London: *Love of Life* was read, discussed, and related to London's life, adventures, and apparent philosophies.

Mark Twain: "The Notorious Jumping Frog of Calaveras County" served as the vehicle for considering the author's humor and reflections upon local color.

Kenneth Grahame: *Wind in the Willows* was read in its entirety. Analysis was directed toward the questions: "What makes the characters memorable?" "Why has this book been characterized as a classic?" and "Can a novel be fiction and still be realistic and lifelike?"

Robert Frost: Poems read included "Mending Wall," "The Road Not Taken," and "Tree at My Window."

Edward Lear: Selections from *Complete Nonsense* were read with particular attention given to his limericks, which served as stimulation for student attempts at limerick writing.

e. e. cummings: Selected poems were the basis for an understanding of the poet's unusual style and his approaches to the use of unusual language and punctuation.

Bret Harte: His poetry served to illustrate the period and environment in which he traveled. "Has his humor survived the passage of time or was it situational?"

Theater: Greek and Elizabethan theater methods offered specific characteristics for comparisons to contemporary productions.

Ballet: Discussions and study of ballet as an art were complemented by pictorial and recorded musical works of some of the major composers.

Opera: As part of the many concerts and demonstrations sponsored by the Fine Arts Summer School, classes saw the one act opera, *Rita,* by Donizetti. To further demonstrate the characteristics of this composer, students heard recorded selections from *Lucia di Lammermoor*. Selected arias from Gounod's *Faust* were presented, and Menotti's *Amahl and the Night Visitors* was offered in its entirety as the students studied the libretto.

Classical music: Awareness and appreciation again characterized the listening and subsequent discussions of: Rossini's

William Tell Overture, Bach's Brandenburg Concerto No. 2, Handel's *Water Music,* Copland's *Billy the Kid,* Tchaikovsky's *Swan Lake,* and Mendelssohn's *Midsummer Night's Dream.*

Jazz: After group orientations and appreciation sessions, Phil Elwood, KPFA jazz commentator, spoke to the students on the background of jazz, history of the phonograph, and recording techniques. In addition, various jazz styles were compared to classical music.

Folk music: Learnings were addressed to the questions: "What is folk music?" "How is it created and by whom?" "How is it performed?" "What instruments are used?" and "Should one try to compare different singers' interpretations of the same song?" A study of various musical instruments played in folk music expanded the dimensions of this medium. Recordings of specific artists were analyzed (see section on Resources): Sam Hinton, Pete Seeger, Mike Seeger, Mance Lipscomb, Jean Richie, Leadbelly, Oscar Brand, Joan Baez, Limelighters, Mainer's Mountaineers, and Peter, Paul and Mary.

Language development (English): To demonstrate changes in the English language, 12th, 14th, and 20th century descriptions and word usages were presented in chart (comparison) form. Selections were read from works of John Gomer, 14th century poet, and from the middle-English text, *Gawain and the Green Knight.*

Religion and Philosophy: Hindu and Buddhist tenets were described and discussed.

Propaganda: By examining basic propaganda techniques in fields such as politics and advertising, students were encouraged to identify the obvious and subtle pressures exerted upon the public through these approaches: plain folks, bandwagon, testimonial, transfer, guilt and virtue by association, glittering generalities, and name calling. Several of the pupils contributed newspaper, magazine, radio, and TV advertising materials for classroom analysis.

Resources — If alertness to and awareness of the students' surroundings were to be encouraged, it was assumed that real, concrete, representative exposures would convey the message to them. All field studies were preceded by preparatory learnings and followed by evaluative sessions in an attempt to integrate the concrete experience into meaningful thinking. Five examples of field studies follow.

A folk music festival, conducted on the Berkeley campus of the University of California, brought together many of the authentic (less compromising) artists in the field. The students attended a performance of folk music followed by a panel discussion by the singers who described their backgrounds, methods they had used in collecting their songs, and reasons for their selecting folk music as a performing art.

Another trip to the University of California enabled the students to see a photographic exhibition, "The World of Werner Bischof." In a tour of the University library the group studied card catalogs and IBM checking system and saw a Robert Frost exhibit. During a tour of Bancroft Library students saw Drake's plate and an 8th century record of a pre-Spanish local war. In the Rare Book Room the University staff had prepared a display of pages from the Gutenburg Bible, illuminated texts, original manuscripts and maps, an edition of *Gulliver's Travels*, the smallest book in the world, and other incunabula. In the microfilm room the library staff demonstrated the microfilming process and related it to library research functions. Berkeley bookstores were visited for art prints and paperbacks.

The world of architecture, studied in the classroom, was illustrated through inspections of Marin County Center, San Rafael, which gave the students an orientation to the genius of Frank Lloyd Wright. San Francisco's Palace of Fine Arts and churches in the immediate area were viewed and discussed, and the Greek Theatre (Berkeley) architecture served as a contrast to other designs experienced on the trip.

Sonoma County's contributions to California history and literature were illustrated by visits to Jack London State Park, the Harazthy Winery, the Sonoma Mission, other historically significant buildings in Sonoma Square, and Vallejo's home.

The Palace of the Legion of Honor in San Francisco gave further opportunities for art appreciation and understanding. Collections and exhibitions studied included 18th century paintings, rococo works, medieval art, sculpture by Rodin, period furniture, and the visiting British Chatsworth collection of drawings by masters such as Holbein, Da Vinci, Raphael, Rubens, Van Dyke, and Rembrandt.

Program Evaluation (Pupils) — Teacher observations of pupil behavior and open-ended interviews served as vehicles for evaluating pupil responses to the session. Although initially many students were openly skeptical about parental interest in having them participate, the group was in essential agreement that the experiences had been exciting and intellectually gratifying. In most of the evaluative comments the students described their excitement in terms of learnings not previously encountered.

The group interviews did not differentiate between pupil reactions to total exposures and their responses to independent study projects. Pupil responses seemed to fall into four general incidence areas:

1. Increased knowledge beyond a superficial awareness of the environment.
2. A new perception of self through exploration of new and varied content.
3. The discovery of new personal interests.
4. Daily anticipation, broadened minds, and unusual methods of learning.

Program Evaluation (Parents) — Four weeks after the close of the summer session, a questionnaire was sent to the parents of participating students. It attempted to elicit parental perceptions about the program. Tabulated responses showed that parents were aware of changes in their children. Comments included an increased desire to learn, a better grasp of "living," increased curiosity, recognition of specific aspects of culture, and more awareness of individual potentialities.

Program Evaluation (Teachers) — Generally, the teachers were confronted by a conflict in their program planning — a conflict that could be described as "Should we offer exposures on a broad basis or should the students experience research and study in depth?" Undoubtedly because of their desire to explore many different areas according to their interests, compromise characterized their planning, and thus their conflicts continued throughout the session. They found that the shotgun approach captured the interests and imagination of the wide range of backgrounds represented in the student population.

Unequivocally, the instructors enjoyed their teaching experience. Although the field studies had an impact, they would limit them in the future. More resource persons would be utilized. The course was stimulating and challenging enough for the majority of the students as long as open-ended questions were used. Parental involvement should be expanded. Finally the teachers saw possibilities and implications for the curriculum during the conventional school year: groupings by common interest regardless of age, independent study, integration of humanities into several areas of the curriculum, and modified team-teaching possibilities. The teachers felt that the original objectives were satisfactorily met and hoped the summer program would continue.

Frances Hufford [*]
Fourth-, fifth-, and sixth-grade junior humanities; concentrates on famous people who have contributed to literature, music, art, architecture, and philosophy; calendar approach.

History and Rationale — In 1967 the fourth-grade teachers at Dale Mabry school set up a team-teaching approach for their work for the year. Two teachers taught several levels of math, two teachers taught enriched reading and math, and the writer taught two 45-minute periods of junior humanities.

In general, the humanities cover a large variety of subjects such as English, philosophy, history, classics, political science, economics, languages, anthropology, sociology, the fine arts, and many more. For elementary boys and girls, the approach to and the definition of the humanities should be simple. Humanities is the study of the lives and works of men and women who have contributed, or who are now contributing, to the advance of civilization through literature, music, art, architecture, and philosophy.

Objectives

MAIN OBJECTIVES	BEHAVIORAL OBJECTIVES
To enable boys and girls to live fuller, more meaningful	The child participates in musical activities, in groups or

---

[*] Mrs. Hufford is now at Morgan Woods Elementary School and is using this approach for Junior humanities with fourth-, fifth-, and sixth-graders.

lives by learning to appreciate good music, to enjoy and
remember beautiful poetry,
and to recognize excellence
in art, whether it be in painting, sculpture, or architecture.

alone; he reads poems he has
learned and enjoys reciting
poems he has learned; he
participates in choral reading. He learns to look at a
painting and perceive color,
shape, and movement, to dis-
tinguish a realistic painting
from a non-objective painting, and recognizes the artist's motive in trying to help
us understand the wonder
and beauty of the world
around us. He learns to identify the architecture and architects in his own community and to enjoy the study,
in general, of classical and
modern architecture and architects.

To understand some of the
teachings of great philosophers.

The child understands the
meaning of the term philosophy and appreciates and enjoys the wisdom gleaned
from great philosophers.

To furnish a foundation for
the cultural background necessary to the young child's
educational progress and to
his wise and advantageous
use of leisure time.

The child recognizes good
reading material and desires
to spend his leisure time
reading and in pursuing
other cultural activities.

To teach boys and girls to
observe, to read, to think,
and to learn from the experi-

The child is able, through research, reports, and reading
to develop an appreciation

MAIN OBJECTIVES	BAHAVIORAL OBJECTIVES
ences of those who have left their "footprints on the sands of time."	of the accomplishments of great people in the past and present.
To extend the school curriculum to correlate humanities with basic classroom instruction.	The child recognizes the correlation with other subjects by orally and graphically relating ideas, i.e., Robert Frost to New England, James Whitcomb Riley to Indiana; and Grant Wood to Iowa.

Approach — The plan that has proved successful for presenting junior humanities is a calendar approach. Children are fascinated by birthdays and are eager to learn of famous people with whom they share birthdays. This plan reaches out in all directions, like the spokes in a wheel, and is held together by the tight rim of the children's interest.

To draw attention to the architecture, art, literature, music, and philosophy to be studied during the month, bulletin boards are prepared to point up people, places and things. The children are encouraged to supplement the suggestions given with pictures, poems, records, and various other related subject matter.

Two other bulletin boards play an important part in the humanities program: the current event board and the Laffin' Place. Boys and girls are expected to find newspaper articles pertinent to what is being studied and to cut out cartoons and comic strips and bring them to class.

Dates should not be too important a part of junior humanities, but a simple time line divided into half centuries — the children writing in the names of people as they study them — is helpful. A time line for periods may also be used: Egypt, Greece, Rome, Byzantine, Romanesque, Gothic,

Italian Renaissance, French Renaissance, English Renaissance, 17th, 18th, and 19th century American, and so on.

Requirements — All students in the fourth-, fifth-, and sixth-grades are involved in the humanities course. Humanities classes are held for one 45-minute period daily.

Boys and girls are expected to look up the famous people studied and make reports and book reports on them. Each student is required to make a scrap book with sections for architecture, art, music, literature, and philosophy.

Every boy and girl participates in a humanities program with choral reading, music, and discussions of art and artists. In so far as possible, each boy and girl participates in a play as an actor or backstage man.

Materials — Since choral reading and poetry are integral parts of junior humanities, it is necessary to have many volumes of poetry on hand. The boys and girls are taught poetry by rote — the teacher reciting a line or two at a time and the children repeating the lines.

Music to listen to and music to sing is an important part of junior humanities. It is necessary to have a good record player and as many recordings as possible. However, the boys and girls bring records from home to supplement the study of composers and compositions.

Films and filmstrips are available on people of note in architecture, art, music, literature, and philosophy. Creative dramatics are an important part of the humanities program. Costumes, props, make-up, and lighting require initiative on the part of teacher and children.

Ceramics, sculpture, and other activities require appropriate materials.

Resources — People from the community give talks and demonstrations on the various humanities areas studied. Guided tours of places of interest in the city provide enriching experiences.

Brother Mario Sartori
Seventh and eighth grades; flexible, changing course based on relationships between environment, custom, historical events, and the ideal individual; filmmaking and video workshop.

Rationale — The humanities program at Iona aims to develop a reflective and critical attitude toward the world around our students. The primary focus is a study of environment as a force that greatly affects people. Attention is also given to the study of varying ideals of behavior in different environmental situations. We try to give particular attention to the contemporary world and encourage our students to analyze it in terms of its forces and ideals.

Students and Instruction — The course is open to all students in the eighth-grade and is guided primarily by an individual instructor. Guest speakers and periods of team-teaching are incorporated into the schedule. We have an all male student body, generally aged 12 to 13, and have found it easy to split the course into two classes of a homogeneous nature.

Course of Study — Our course has changed extensively in the four years it has been in existence. These changes were made in response to practical considerations arising from the age and type of students with whom we work and also in part from an expansion of our theoretical framework. Our first program was basically an epoch approach, dealing with the ancient, medieval, Renaissance, and modern periods. We attempted to ascertain the basic ideology and flavor of each period and to look for differences and relationships between periods. It worked, but our feelings were that it was too cerebrally focused to be of any true affective value to the child. This went against one of our basic tenets — that the humanities should reach the total person. A partial solution to the problem was discovered in our second year. We retained the core material from the previous year and added individual units on subjects suggested by the class as worthy of further study. In this way the students established the pattern and the emphasis for the course, yet the formal epoch approach still knitted the various parts into a unity.

In 1968 we realized that studying historical periods as such lacked true purpose for the age groups with whom we were dealing, so the course was reorganized on an anthropological basis. We began our study with an investigation of how environment affects man. We used a text[1] that examined four primitive tribes from vastly differing physical surroundings and sought to discover how their environments helped to mold their customs, religious beliefs, and conceptions of the ideal man. Next we considered the basic periods of Western historical development. Using epics as our starting points, we tried to ascertain the relationships among environment, custom, historical events, and the ideal individual. We concentrated particularly on the ancient, medieval (both high and low) and Renaissance periods. When we reached the modern period, however, we didn't use the epic form to give us a picture of the times, but rather contemporary art and artifacts. We focused on advertising, rock lyrics, films, and short stories to find for ourselves the major currents of the times. Near the end of the year, we also began filmmaking as a substitute and complement to written and oral expression, both of which were stressed during earlier parts of the year. In the future we plan to keep the basic course essentially the

---

1. Lisitzky, Gene. *Four Ways of Being Human.* New York: Viking Press, 1964.

same but to include some new texts and to use video-tape equipment in addition to student-made films.

To support student readiness for the program, we have found it necessary to change the seventh-grade English syllabus so that students will be exposed to the basic literary and media forms before being asked to examine and correlate these in grade eight. The seventh-grade student now concentrates on literary genre, particularly the novel, play, and short story. Film is introduced as a form of artistic expression and a viable means of communication. The basic attitudes and techniques of film study are also covered. At present the humanities course is scheduled only for grades seven and eight, in terms of preparation and actual material.

The humanities approach, as distinct from a separate subject matter, is an important element of the school from grade one. This is an educational approach that synthesizes various disparate subjects into a correlated framework before presentation. It is our hope that a formal period of humanities can be established throughout the primary grades. This program would follow the project approach in which an individual aspect of man and his relation to the world would be studied each year. The course in the seventh- and eighth-grades would attempt to correlate and expand on these earlier units. This will take time to establish, but we see it as valuable. Planning has already begun to expand the program.

Resources — Hopefully our new video workshop will help make the expansion of the program to the lower grades more practical in terms of resource materials and teacher exchange possibilities.

The completion of a large separate library collection, which is being assembled to support this curriculum, is important to our plans. Though extensive use is already being made of this collection by students, its completion will make it possible for us to prepare schedules in the upper grades for more independent study units in the humanities. This development would flow naturally from the present structure of the program, where each unit is culminated or centered around a student project. Independent study[2] could be done as a continuation of themes brought up in class as part of a unit or as discovered by the child himself in research for his project.

Materials — A detailed course description including recommended texts and materials is in preparation. Teachers interested in receiving this information should address their requests to the writer, Iona Grammar School, Stratton Road, New Rochelle, New York 10804.

Conclusion — We must stress the flexibility basic to our program. Change is essential to a good humanities program. Unless our scope of instruction fulfills needs and meets students halfway, it has little possible effect. We must work to affect the child on the human level; all other education is cant. We must be willing to search for ways to relate to *today's* students. Since needs and interests are not constant, neither can our materials and approach be so well organized and structured that it is impossible to alter one facet without destroying some vast synthesis we have built up for ourselves.

Finally, it has amazed us how much we can do for and with children when we use a basic humanities approach. Perhaps the method makes our true educational aim more possible — to make man conscious of the dignity and responsibility of his humanity.

2. Our concept of independent study and criteria for implementing it effectively is based on a book by Frank Brown, *Education by Appointment — New Approaches to Independent Study*. West Nyack, N.Y.: Parker Publishing Co., 1968.

Delores Minor
Junior high; one-semester televised series, *Of Cabbages and Kings*, with 36 25-minute programs; concentrates on self-identification by enriching literary experiences; thematically structured; conceptual and inductive approach; team-teaching.

Rationale and Objectives — The Detroit public school system is beginning its fourth year of a one-semester junior high school televised humanities series. Initially supported by a federal grant under Title I of ESEA, the series, *Of Cabbages and Kings*, is intended to be something more than a show-and-tell literature course accompanied by the conventional emphasis upon facts and details. Rather, it is a humanities-oriented series designed to help students explore and concentrate affectively on the basic humanistic theme of self-identification.

The series was designed to enable students to develop a cultural awareness of themselves and others through enriching literary experiences.

Approach — To a large extent the television medium dictated the approach used in the series as did the aim, rationale, and composition of the student body. Consisting of 36 programs, each in 25-minute segments, the series is thematically structured under units of humor, folklore, self-image, adventure, biography, family, poetry, mystery, frontier, drama, imagination and reality, and teen renaissance. Each of these units, with from two to four individually contained programs, encourages students to respond to the theme of self-identification.

The approach is conceptual and inductive with more questions asked than answers given. Using this Socratic method, the series avoids ready-made interpretations so that students can advance their own understandings and conclusions.

Revolving around a television format specifically geared for the adolescent junior high school student, programs emphasize enjoyment and appreciation of literary experiences. Telecasts generally focus on an opening teaser to arouse interest and proceed to dramatizations, pantomimes, and interpretive readings of literature. Each of these vignettes embraces the specific objective of the program and more broadly seeks to help students discover the relationship of the literary experience to themselves. With music, art, and dance an integrated part of the series, each literary selection is introduced and followed up by leading questions asked by the host in a 30 second to one minute on-camera span to help students discover for themselves the essence of the activity. By using this method, the series ultimately hopes to help students learn the art and skill of inquiry, of discourse and dialogue, and of independent study and learning.

Students and Instructors — Although *Of Cabbages and Kings* was planned to relate to culturally disadvantaged students in 16 specific junior high schools, grades seven to nine, weekly evaluations and observations throughout the semester revealed that the series can be effective in all types of school situations as well as with different categories and grade levels of junior high school students.

The course is repeated each semester and is a part of the regular English curriculum. As such, students taking the course receive five hours of English credit.

The series is a team-teaching project. Long before the series went into production, the individuals in charge of the program had firsthand information from teachers, students, administrators, and librarians in each of the original 16 schools on composition of students and their favorite units of study, most popular books, reading levels, and ability groupings, if any. During the video-taping, the on-camera host depended on immediate constructive feedback from the classroom or viewing teacher and his students for revision purposes.

Requirements — Students are not required to read the literature prior to the telecasts because of the low reading levels of students for whom the series was designed. However, with interest generated by means of dramatizations and other visuals, students are stimulated to read not only the works dramatized but other selections that relate to the themes of the units.

Activities — After students view the 25-minute telecasts two days a week, the remaining 25 minutes of the class periods and the remaining three days of the week are spent in such activities as students: discussing ideas that emanated from telecasts; formulating personal concepts; engaging in their own interpretations of literature, freely integrating music, art, and dance; working on individual or class projects; writing short papers; reading; viewing related media materials; and, with the teacher, preparing the class for the next telecast or unit theme.

Materials and Resources — In addition to viewing the video-tapes, students have access in their classroom to over one hundred paperbacks that include literature dramatized on the series as well as books related to the unit themes. The second supplement to which students have access is a multi-media kit, compartmentalized to correspond to the theme of each of the units in the series. Included among the media are pictures, maps, books, photographs, charts, articles, films, tapes, filmstrips, records, pamphlets, and transparencies. One of the two additional compartments of the kit contains multi-media materials that relate in general to all of the units; the second additional compartment, void of materials, is an open invitation to students and teachers to add their own media.

Students themselves provide the essential visualization of the telecasts in their dramatizations, dances, pantomimes, and interpretive readings.

Three other resources include: a teacher's teleguide for the series, separate teacher's guides for the supplementary paperbacks, and the multi-media kit.

Conclusions — Too often teachers stifle creative energies of students by giving the proverbial check-up or review test to ascertain what facts were gleaned and remembered. Since the emphasis of the series is on students' perceptiveness, their personal interpretations of selections, and their own value judgments, not on facts and details or right or wrong answers, no written objective-type examinations are given for the course. Instead, evaluation should be based primarily on students' formal and informal oral work during the semester and on their written responses to concepts presented. Since the emphasis is more on affective than cognitive skills, teachers should concern themselves more with the *what* rather than the *how* of students' writings.

At the beginning students may be shy about expressing themselves; therefore, teachers are encouraged to be patient and skillful in bringing them into the activities. In the end students may discover that it can be a rich and rewarding experience to concern themselves about the concept of self, to think seriously, perhaps for the very first time, about who they are, what kind of persons they are, and how experiences from literature relate to them personally. If students can eventually evolve a personal concept of self-identification based on the units in the series, then the teacher takes "delight in the thing just because it is what it is."

Susan Jacoby and Richard Lavigne
Seventh- and eighth-grade accelerated students; art and English with some music and social studies; stresses self-expression; aimed to develop children as artists, critics, and scholars; thematic questions; filmmaking and field trips.

History — In 1969 a humanistically oriented and correlated art and English program was introduced to an accelerated group of eighth-grade students at the John Read Middle School. It was offered with the hope that these students might develop keener awareness of the interrelationship of these two disciplines and in turn recognize that all knowledge has continuous and interwoven threads. The success of this program led to the development of a similar course of study for the seventh-grade the following year. At that time the project was funded by the State of Connecticut through Title V (P.L. 89–10), Small Demonstration Centers.

Like humanities studies at many other schools throughout the country, the humanities course at John Read generated an enthusiasm among students that was contagious. The course was offered for a full year and was given 7–12 periods a week, meeting back to back. While it was formally offered only to accelerated students, the interrelationships of the disciplines found its way to most other seventh- and eighth-grade classes.

Rationale and Objectives — Why a humanities course? Tuning in students to the vast means of communication available to them was one major objective of the program. No longer were they confined to the traditional methods of expression — written or oral. The stress was on creative, alive, consistent, and constant reactions to the various media — photographs, books, tapes, records, films, video-tape, or dimensional objects. The correlated humanities curriculum was an attempt to prepare students to cope with the freedom, fluidity, mobility, and challenge that will face them as they mature in a progressive technological society. For this reason, self-expression was emphasized.

A curriculum was designed to expose students to a variety of materials to help them see themselves in a fuller perspective. To develop children as artists, critics, and scholars was a major goal — as artists, so that they might gain confidence in their ability to see things creatively and in new ways; as critics, so that they might see their own virtues and shortcomings as well as those of others; and as scholars, so that they might happily and successfully pursue intellectual goals.

Despite the importance of the aforementioned objectives, the most important objective of all was to help children grow and respond as human beings. The curriculum was structured to bring their world into the classroom, which served as a lively forum for debate, discussion, discovery, and development. With an eye on the past, a view of the present, and a concern for the future, the curriculum unfolded throughout the year within a general predetermined framework. Every activity, however, was conceived with the process of exploration, experimentation, and discovery clearly in mind.

Approach and Course of Study — Both the seventh- and eighth-grade curricula were based on a thematic questions approach. The course opened with an inward look as students groped for and grappled with the problems of self-identification — Who am I? From a unit with a definite personal approach, they moved on to view other men, other times, and other ideas. "How was man conceived by short story writers, novelists, television script writers, dramatists, historians, sociologists, anthropologists, artists, and film-makers?" "Did man of the past have any positive link with man today — man tomorrow?" "Were there ideas that concerned and troubled man throughout his history?" While these questions were considered carefully, they were considered in relationship to thematic units rather than chronologically.

Though not formally incorporated in the course of study, both music and social studies were integrated into the seventh-grade humanities program. As social studies covered world geography, it often proved relevant. Music could hardly be ignored as it played a vital role in the study of man; thus it too found a permanent place in the program.

The following comprised the basic units of study in the seventh-grade program:

Who Am I: A unit designed to help students develop a positive self-image and a better understanding of themselves.

The Short Story: A unit designed to help students explore man as perceived by short story writers, to examine the conflicts of man, and to express their ideas about this literary form.

The Living Stage: A unit designed to familiarize students with all facets of the stage — the reading and writing of drama, costuming, staging, and so on. Trips to the theater were included. A sub-unit dealt entirely with Shakespeare and his world.

The Hollywood Approach: A unit designed to analyze and make film.

The Family: A unit designed to examine the basic social force in contemporary society.

Students were involved in a comprehensive study of the short story and read ancient literature as well as current works. They illustrated their literary explorations with various artistic media and examined the basic conflicts of man as presented by the writers. At the same time they examined ideas, concepts, and values — their own and others. Later on they studied the stage as another means of looking at man. They became involved in the theater as a means of expression through the production of student works. They talked to people in the community whose life was the stage, and they attended performances at the nearby Stratford Shakespeare Theater as well as Lincoln Center.

Probably the most successful and fruitful attempts to examine man and his world came through the study of contemporary media — film and photography. Film was studied as an art, as a form of literature, and as a social commentary. Students viewed both short and feature films almost daily for a period of several months. They wrote scripts, shot film, edited film, and created sound tracks. They wrote critically of what they saw, spoke critically of what they did, and expressed their ideas on celluloid. They worked alone. They worked in small groups. They worked as a large group. They set and met goals. They talked and analyzed and did.

To live in this modern world, which McLuhan has described as a "global village," a child must learn his role and how to communicate with ease. The program at John Read attempted to meet these goals by providing one small injection of humanistically oriented work to show that several disciplines can be more meaningful when studied together. John Ciardi once said that a fool could look at the world and see nothing while the right person could look at a cell, a leaf, or a moth and see the universe. This was a goal of the course at John Read—perceptive children.*

Objectives

1. To develop a significant and keen awareness of the interrelationships of disciplines as well as an awareness of past, present, and future.
2. To foster a transfer of this awareness and its immediate and long-range applicability to the total environment. The eventual outcome of this awareness is a reuniting of shredded knowledge.
3. To strengthen the ability to conceptualize.
4. To develop skills in the disciplines and skills that bridge the gaps between them.
5. To fully utilize the learning methods of exploration, experimentation, and discovery.
6. To develop the ability to think critically, analytically, intuitively, and creatively when solving problems.
7. To promote an enrichment of verbal and visual communication.
8. To experiment with materials feasible in a curriculum approach of this nature.
9. To help children develop as more perceptive and aware human beings.
10. To grow and learn from each other.
11. To develop a keener insight in curriculum planning among teachers and to become more familiar with other disciplines outside one's own speciality.

---

* Though this program is no longer in existence at John Read, the interrelated work described remains vital to the ongoing teaching there.

Materials — Following is a partial list of some materials used: *Books: A Christmas Carol, Androcles and the Lion, A Midsummer Night's Dream, Sunrise at Campobello, The Miracle Worker, Diary of Anne Frank, Short Stories to Enjoy, Short Stories to Remember, Twenty Grand,* and *Exploring the Film.*

Assorted records, tapes, and approximately 50 films, including: *Timepiece, The Chicken, Toys, An Occurrence at Owl Creek Bridge, Diary of Anne Frank, Neighbors, Clay, Glass, Begone Dull Care, The Railrodder, Laurel and Hardy, Sunday Lark,* and *I Wonder Why.*

Marilyn Amdur

Three-year social studies and English courses for grades six–eight, correlated with other subjects whenever appropriate; man-centered, world-view, multi-media approach and activities.

Rationale — In a world of fast moving changes, both wondrous and terrible, we search for happiness with a kind of desperation. If we are so fortunate to have public schooling, then why not explore the possibility of revitalizing the social sciences? With a humanities approach, we can see the totality of man in a cultural setting. We can creep inside him and feel the impact of forces from within and without. With sensory involvement, we are the man — coping, creating, relating, reacting. In such a way we hope to better understand his needs and our needs so that, as unstatistical beings, we can hope to hold the beauty and strength of the human fabric together and, moreover, interweave our own distinctive patterns and colors.

History and Approach — During the summer months of 1967, a team of teachers met to consider the redirection of the social studies program in grades six, seven, and eight. Their experience included teaching English, art, music, and library skills as well as social studies, and they were all sensitive to the interrelationships of these disciplines in living. They felt that teaching about life should involve all these subjects simultaneously and that the program should be man-centered with a world view rather than be "western civ" oriented.

The principal challenge was how to insure not only intellectual understanding but empathy in the largest possible measure. It was strongly felt that an initial study of human emotions would provide the unifying element of contact needed with all peoples everywhere. Thus, a unit on the emotions was devised as a base for the whole course of study. As each area of the world was explored, one country was investigated in depth, so that man could be studied in relation to his environment, fellow man, individual expression, and cultural heritage in the most personal way possible. The multi-media approach was emphasized for more effective sensory and intellectual involvement. Outside field trips and visitors to the classroom injected additional realism.

In each unit of study ample attention was devoted to the development of the knowledge and basic skills that are needed to support rational thought and expression.

The program spans a three-year period of time. At present all sixth-grades are using the humanities direction in social studies. The social studies teacher, however, works closely with teachers of English, art, music, physical education, and home economics whenever their particular disciplines can add breadth and depth to the study of a given society so that students have meaningful experience in "other rooms."

The original two pilot classes at the sixth-grade level last year are now experiencing humanities in the same vein in the seventh-grade. Hopefully, these same two original classes in humanities will pilot at the eighth-grade level next year, while all sixth- and seventh-grades participate in the humanities.

All teachers involved continue to carefully evaluate our progress throughout the year. Summers are used for more extensive planning. We dare to think that "we are the music makers . . ." at the Memorial Junior School!

Students and Instructors — All students in grade levels six, seven, and eight will be involved in the humanities starting

1970–71. Dialogue with primary grades and the senior high school will be maintained so that the continuity of program is assured.

The English and social studies teachers plan together. Teachers in art, music, home economics, and other areas of curriculum that enrich cultural studies are consulted to provide simultaneous experiences.

Requirements — The students are involved with the following activities during the year: individual research and reports; creative art and music projects; family living experiences with preparation of native dishes and menus, study of dress and home furnishings, discussion of values in the home; and creative dramatics or role-playing to bring cultural study to life.

Course of Study —

Basic Concepts Developed Throughout Programs

I. Man's relation to his natural world—his physical needs and how they are met: food, clothing, shelter, and defense
II. Man's need to express himself
   A. Religion: explanation of environment and superior force(s)
   B. Aesthetic expression: art, music, architecture, dance, sculpture, crafts, and inventions
   C. Literary expression: drama, literature, poetry, and folk tales
III. Man's need to relate to his fellow man
   A. Family life
   B. Communal life: law, trade, government, and commerce
IV. Man's attachment to his cultural heritage

Course of Study for Sixth-Grade

I. Emotions common to man
II. Relation of man to modern times
III. Relation of man to ancient times: man in the prehistoric world, man in Mesopotamia, man in Greece in depth, man in Egypt, man in Rome, and man in Ghana in depth

Course of Study for Seventh-Grade

I. Restate emotions of man in his modern surroundings
II. Relation of man to Africa and Kenya in depth
III. Relation of man to Asia and China in depth
IV. Relation of man to Europe and Germany in depth

Course of Study for Eighth-Grade

I. Restate human emotions in terms of current "happenings"
II. Relations of man to exploration: Viking, French, Spanish, Russian, Portuguese, and English
III. Relation of man to colonization: north — Canada, middle — United States, and south — Mexico, Central and South America with Peru in depth.
IV. Relation of man to nation building: United States to 1812, Canada, and Latin America

Scheduling — All humanities classes meet every day during the full year. The sixth- and seventh-grade operate on a block of time basis with the same teachers working with English and social studies. The eighth-grade English and social studies classes are scheduled back to back so that teachers can work together as a team.

Resources and Activities — Teachers and students are actively involved with any part of the school and community, as well as with people and places outside of the area, where reinforcement of study is appropriate. This is particularly important to keep the human element alive.

There is a great deal of expression in drama, poetry, music, art, and home economics projects, field trips, and museum visits. Frequent and varied performances in the arts are brought to the school in general assembly programs.

There is a filmmaking program that is very popular. An annual social studies symposium in which children present other cultures creatively for the community is a high point. Exchange visits in which students at a school in Newark come to us and our orchestral students go to the Newark school for program presentations brings together students of diverse backgrounds. Involvement is stressed wherever and whenever possible with any part of the program that will sensitize the children to values and achievements on the part of others.

Since resourcefulness, curiosity, and flexibility are encouraged, the following resources are used: books, films, filmstrips, tapes, records, slides, TV, graphics, and realia; excellent library resources; and extensive use of outside references.

Susan Nelson and Maryann Tressler

Ninth-grade, inter-city girls; one-semester course of three consecutive daily periods; integrates history, English, art, music, dance, drama, foods, clothing, science, philosophy, and economics by studying four cultures; parental involvement encouraged.

History — The humanities course taught at Lulu Diehl Junior High School, located in the inner-city of Cleveland, includes a heterogeneous group of 55 girls. In order to have three consecutive periods, a block of two hours and 15 minutes, these students are scheduled for English, social studies, and study hall. The class meets in a large room that can easily accommodate all the various methods applied in the course. To encourage parent involvement, a meeting was held for parents at the Cleveland Museum of Art to introduce them to the humanities concept and the unique nature of this program in a junior high school. A sample lecture and art presentation was given, and the parents who attended this orientation program showed great interest throughout the semester. The funds for this semester course were raised by the entire student body in a school-sponsored candy sale.

Objectives —

1. To make more relevant the various disciplines by integrating history, literature, art, music, dance, drama, foods, clothing, science, philosophy, and economics into one course.

2. To present opportunities for evaluation and objective analysis of various civilizations and cultures.
3. To emphasize the different responses of man and to discover the overall universality of mankind.
4. To prepare students for high school by developing their skills in the following areas: lecture method and note-taking, organized discussion for the expression of ideas through small group interchanges, independent study, library usage, active participation in the arts, objectives consideration of things and people, and evaluations of field trips, resource persons, and motion pictures.

Approach — The study of four cultures focused on answering basic questions:

1. What does man do to physically survive (geography, foods, clothing, economics)?
2. How do people organize their societies so that they can live harmoniously (politics, government, sociology, history)?
3. How does man attempt to explain the unknown (science, religion, philosophy)?
4. How does man express his ideas and emotions (art, music, dance, drama, literature)?

Staff — An English teacher and a social studies teacher taught this course for all three periods. In addition three teachers in training with the Teacher Corps were assigned so that the students would be introduced to the various backgrounds of a number of teachers and so that group discussions among 11 pupils could be supervised. School faculty from different departments enriched each phase of study in their various disciplines. They gave lectures, demonstrations, and occasionally led discussion.

Activities — Believing that students must be included in planning and presenting various aspects of the materials, whenever possible opportunities were given for student leadership. In addition to faculty and outside speakers, students delivered lectures. Other student-conducted activities included large class debates and discussions, plays, group presentations of student research, and independent study. Student-oriented activities included role-playing, small group discussions, art projects, and dance demonstrations. In addition, the following field trips broadened student experience: Cleveland Public Library, Cleveland City Hall, Humanities Conference at Baldwin-Wallace College, Glenville High School production of *West Side Story*, May show of modern art, and Cleveland Museum of Art.

Requirements — Each student was required to purchase a spiral notebook to facilitate note-taking. The student made a pocket on the inside of the back cover to keep all dittoed materials. These notebooks were collected regularly to insure meaningful note-taking. In addition to other means of evaluation, objective and essay unit tests and a final oral and written examination were administered. Concepts, rather than rote regurgitation, were stressed. Most important, however, each student was required to complete a study of one culture not included in the curriculum and to submit a written 2,000 word term paper and a visual project, such as a model village or native costume. These visual projects were displayed at a Humanities Fair as part of a school open house.

Course of Study — The four units of study considered were:

Ancient Greece: This culture was selected not only because it was included in the ninth-grade English curriculum, but also because it was during this period that western civilization, as we know it, originated. This unit was six weeks in length.

Ancient and Modern West Africa: The emergence of new independent nations and the worldwide movement for human rights make knowledge of these cultures an essential part of the study of any well-educated American student. This unit was four weeks in length.

Civil War America, 1840–1877: Since this period in American history introduces civil conflict within our nation, and again the human rights movement, this unit is most relevant to pupils today. Three weeks were spent on this unit of study.

Modern America, 1920–1969: Since this is the time in which we are living, this culture is most meaningful as it introduces modern American government and thought, part of the ninth-grade social studies curriculum. This unit was five weeks in length.

Materials

Readings: All or part of the following were read: *Your Life as a Citizen* by Smith and Bruntz, *The Odyssey, The Iliad, The Trojan Women, The Aeneid,* book 2, Greek philosophical writings and poetry, *African Treasury* edited by Langston Hughes, *West Side Story* by Laurents, modern American poetry, excerpts from Hemingway and Fitzgerald, *Red Badge of Courage, Selected Poems* by Whitman, "Jim Baker's Blue-jay Yarn" by Twain, "The Cask of Amontillado" by Poe, writings on slavery by ex-slaves and observers, *Stride Toward Freedom* by King, and *Awake and Sing* by Odets.

Resource speakers: two West African college students, an authority on West Africa, a former Peace Corpsman stationed in West Africa, a Cleveland teacher at the Museum of Art who was a specialist on West African and Modern American art.

Mannikins: A male and a female mannikin were provided by Sears-Roebuck Co. The figures were dressed by the students in clothing fashions of the culture being studied.

Visual Resources: Motion pictures included: *Humanities* by Clifton Fadiman, *Odyssey* (I, II, and III), *Plato's Apology, Literature in America—Short Story, People of the Congo, Question in Togoland, Victoria Falls, Frederick Douglass, History of the Negro in America* (1619–1860, 1860–1877, and 1877–today), *Mark Twain's America, New England Background of Literature, Stalin,* and *Major Religions.* Slides included: Greek and modern American art and the operetta, *Porgy and Bess.*

Anyone interested in further information regarding humanities at Diehl is invited to write to the authors at Lulu Diehl Junior High School, 1325 Ansel Road, Cleveland, Ohio 44106.

Norman Ward Wilson
"An Image of Man: The Beginning, the Defects, and the Struggle to Be an Individual"; units combine music, art, literature, social studies, and philosophy under English department; team-teaching; stresses perceptual awareness; utilizes electronic environmental learning center for independent study.

Objectives — The underlying purpose of the Burnt Hills humanities program is in the affective rather than the cognitive domain. We feel a person needs to overcome the rapidly increasing pressures of living in a mass-oriented society — a sort of personal survival kit. Philosophically we are committed to a program that is concerned with the following:

1. A study of man's institutions: Through such a program — the study of man's past, his present, his institutions, his artistic endeavors, his philosophies, and his ethics — the student will begin to understand that there is a direction in life, a reason for being, a system of values, and good reasons why.

2. Values and ethics: The program is designed to help the student build his own value system and code of personal ethics through examining differing ethical questions and systems of values.

3. Understanding: The humanities approach is an attempt to bring to the student an understanding that each period has its own peculiar image of man and that whenever a

new period comes into being, a new image of man emerges.

4. Exploration of new ideas: Serving as a medium through which the student may explore new ideas, the program provides opportunities to examine the interrelationships of art, music, the dance, drama, literature, history, and philosophy. It permits the student to pursue man's thoughts and concepts of being.

5. Individual thinking: Individual thinking, both critical and creative, receives primary stress. The mere mastery of unrelated and isolated facts is of little value and is no concern of the program.

6. Mature thinking: The program assists the student to develop mature, responsible thinking, thus bringing new depth and dimension to his thinking.

7. Opportunity to react: It provides opportunities for the student to react, not to analyze; to think, not to memorize; to discuss, not to absorb; to relate, not to compute; to extend, not to pigeonhole; to wonder, not to know.

8. Developing a synthesis: The humanities course is an attempt to help the student make some collective sense out of man's relationship to his universe.

Approach — Impressed by organizational patterns that break down the traditional classroom situation, we built our humanities program around a group of teachers who are responsible for the course. This group is under the direction of the English department chairman. Large group instruction, modular scheduling, small group work, studio situation, and independent study are the means by which the teaching staff present the course. The teaching team is composed of five people: two English teachers, one art teacher, one music teacher, and a media librarian. The team meets twice a week to plan and build the program.

This past year the program was divided into three broad units under the umbrella title of "An Image of Man: The Beginning, the Defects of Man, and the Struggle to Be an Individual." In each unit music, art, literature, social studies, and philosophy were studied. Next year we plan modifications based upon the very excellent work done by the music people at Case Western Reserve University (USOE Project No. H-116). We will divide the program into four general areas:

1. What does music (art, literature, etc.) do?
2. Who is responsible for making it do what it does?
3. How does it do what it does?
4. How has it done what it has done?

These four questions serve as the unifiers of the program. The literary, musical, and artistic compositions studied will change as need demands.

Evaluation — Evaluation of the 60 students in the humanities program (all are average ability) is based on class participation, small group discussions, written work, projects, and oral presentations. Each member of the teaching team helps evaluate the students. The average of these marks is the grade that appears on the student's report card. Because there is no special place for a humanities mark on the card, the mark is assigned to the English area, and the course replaces the regular English program.

Evaluation is a major trouble area. We wish to lessen the pressures of testing and consequently have abolished the traditional ten-week test. Many projects the students work on receive no grade. The evaluation of the students is based upon: written compositions, oral reports, class discussion, independent study projects, quiz and other test-type evaluation instruments, and art and music projects.

Oral participation and project work receive the major emphasis for evaluation. The teachers meet to discuss each student and arrive jointly at a grade for the report card. Someday, perhaps, we will arrive at the point where marks will not be necessary. The work itself will become the reward.

Course of Study and Materials — The course title is "An Image of Man," and the human activities that make man what he is are explored. For example, music and art, as well as literature, are presented more as an expression of man's humanity than as a product of the age that produced them. In the same way we present man's moral and ethical nature and his ability to make choices based on some standard he has chosen. This is consistent with our philosophy of perceptual awareness that forms much of the theoretical basis for the course.

A partial list of the selections and subjects studied is: world mythology, Genesis, Darwin's theory, *The Dawn of Man* (film), "A Youth" (poem), "The New Man" (*Life* reprint), *The Rime of the Ancient Mariner,* "Man" (poem), *Lord of the Flies, A Separate Peace, To Kill a Mockingbird, The Bridge of San Luis Rey, Hiroshima,* "The Sick Rose" (poem), *Out of the Silent Planet,* "The Interlopers," "The Diamond Necklace," "A Slander," "The Telltale Heart," "Paul's Case," "The Ambitious Guest," "The World Is Too Much with Us," "What Have They Done to the Rain?" (modern protest song), "Where Have All the Flowers Gone?" (modern protest song), "Blowing in the Wind" (modern protest song), *Galacidalacidesoxirbunucleicacid* (Dali painting), *Anthem,* "The Parsley Garden," "The Use of Force," "The Open Road," "The Struggle to Be an Individual" (*Life* reprint), and *The Abolition of Man.*

Other art and music works are still being selected. Much of the art work will be activity rather than the study of great works.

One of the unique features of the program is the utilization of both large and small group instruction. Such scheduling provides more flexibility. The arrangement allows guest speakers, films, studio work in dance, art, drama, and television production, and independent study. Small group work involves no more than eight students.

The electronic environmental learning center (with its dial-access retrieval systems, television studio, etc.) at the junior high school was of great use to the students in the program. It is possible for a student or a group of students to dial a film, television program, audio-tape, slide film, filmstrip, or video-tape through the dial-access system. Many of the newer media and materials are used. Such a center provides great opportunity for independent study in the humanities program.

Conclusions — During the process of program evaluation, which is an ongoing process, several significant conclusions were made. This program in the humanities has demonstrated its value to the student participants, and it seems desirable to attempt to maintain its fine features for a third year. Among these are the following:

1. The thematic approach to the study of man is superior to a fragmented approach.
2. The many-faceted approach to the study of a theme (through art, music, literature, history, and philosophy) provides a greater depth and broader base for understanding.
3. Small group work has allowed more individualization in the teaching-learning process.
4. Independent study by pupils has furthered the individualization of education.
5. Students who had generally been shy and reluctant to become involved have been motivated to more academic success.

All these benefits could most likely be achieved within the regular framework of any schedule or class, but they seem to have developed better when the more traditional ways of teaching were somewhat reduced. Yet with this departure came several problems, which cannot be blamed on any one individual, but it is assumed that they can be solved. They have, however, demonstrated a need for more thought, a breathing time, further planning, and experimentation. Among the problems are:

1. Too much free time was scheduled for students (at the senior high level this may not be so much of a problem).
2. There simply was not enough teacher planning time.
3. Content organization should have been done earlier and should have had more relevancy.
4. Scheduling of teacher time, specifically in the areas of art and music, was difficult.
5. Small group work problems occurred because of lack of teacher training in this area.
6. Team personnel problems developed, which is normal when any new organizational patterns are created.

All these problems can be corrected and eliminated in time, but until the teaching staff has become accustomed to using new materials, equipment, and methods and are more ready to accept and support new teaching approaches as well as academic content, we recommend that the present method of teaching of humanities be limited to a modest effort. We can expand as the staff grows in competency.

Our humanities program is practical from the standpoint of our present school organization and personnel. We hope it is a beginning that will influence other areas of the curriculum and will create a total school concern for man and the problems he faces now and in the years ahead.

Roy York, Jr.
Three offerings: (1) two periods per week for
seventh- and eighth-graders (2) eight or nine
weeks as a unit of English 12, and (3) full-
year elective instead of English 12; all use
allied art approach, resource people from the
University, and multi-media.

History and Objectives — In September 1954, the Milne humanities program* was established. Since that time there
have been three types of offerings, all using the allied arts
approach, many audio-visual aids, and no formal textbook.
Milne is a junior-senior high school, grades seven to twelve,
with 72 students in each grade, equally divided between
boys and girls.

The overall aim is to introduce the student to ways he
may have intense, intelligent, independent experience with
the humanities and to stimulate in him a desire to broaden
and deepen his personal enjoyment and critical judgment
of the arts for the remainder of his life.

Approach — Provision is made for structured learning. It
would seem that the wisest practice is to capitalize on every

---

* For further details concerning the humanities at Milne, see Roy
York, Jr., "Notes on Starting a Humanities Course," *The Journal of
Aesthetic Education*, vol. 2, no. 2, pp. 109–116, April 1968, "Humanities for the Superior High School Student," *The School Music
News*, vol. 26, no. 3, pp. 35–6, November 1962, and "Humanities
in the High School," *Music Educators Journal*, vol. 45, no. 4, pp.
44–8, February–March 1959.

available means of interrelating the offerings in a humanities course such as this. Interrelation can be a superb instrument to use in structuring masses of humanistic knowledge. The student should realize that there are certain principles common to all the arts and that whatever understanding he has of one may be used as an entering wedge to the understanding of other arts.

To provide the student with a sturdy trellis on which to wreathe his artistic information, to marshal ideas, beliefs, opinions, and feelings, and to associate facts of the immense world of man's culture, certain fundamental principles are emphasized. These principles—subject, function, medium, organization, style, judgment—as propounded by Dudley and Faricy in their book *The Humanities* (4th ed., New York: McGraw-Hill, 1967) are the unifying strands that run through the course and culminate in the final examination.

Judicious use is made of whatever creditable performing skills the teacher has. An approximate ratio of one lecture session to every three or four periods devoted to class discussion is advocated.

Courses of Study — In the humanities course for grades seven and eight music is taught along with the other major arts of literature, painting, sculpture, and architecture. Large classes, which alternate with physical education, meet for two periods per week throughout the year. Interrelationships, counterparts, and common principles contribute toward a highly integrated course, which is essentially the same as that described below. Here, however, the students are four and five years younger, and one instructor does all the teaching.

A humanities unit is required in English 12. Visiting specialists in music and the visual arts, and sometimes in philosophy and comparative literature, teach the entire senior class for eight or nine weeks. Presentations by these specialists are discussed at weekly smaller group meetings with each of the three regular members of the English teaching team. Literature is taught by the regular team as the need arises throughout the year.

Humanities may be chosen in preference to either of the two other required electives to earn the prescribed twelfth-grade English credit. The optimum class seems to be about 20 students, meeting daily for one (or two) periods throughout the year.

Instructors and Requirements — A staff of three teachers, one each in music, literature, and the visual arts, makes a suitable combination. To supplement the presentations by this regular staff, from five to ten specialists, almost all of whom are professors from the University, meet with the class each year. Ideally all regular staff are present at every plenary class session.

The music and visual arts instructors delve into the great masterpieces in their fields with the utmost freedom. The literature teacher must have the students meet the state requirements for English 12. This he can accomplish within the Milne humanities course framework, with enormous enrichment assists from the music and visual arts staff.

A term paper for each semester, special reports that encourage pursuit of individual interests and needs, active, intelligent class participation, and evaluative procedures designed as fruitful and interesting learning experiences are among the flexible course requirements.

Materials — A balanced diet of a considerable body of essentially unhackneyed works of art is treated in some cases intensively and in others extensively. Masterpieces or historic exemplars of art are studied as often as possible. Free use is made of phonograph recordings, prints, slides, motion pictures, a classroom bulletin board, and libraries — classroom, school, university, city, and state.

The most important field trip is a three-day humanities pilgrimage to New York City. The cream of the city's cultural offerings considered most valuable for twelfth-graders is served up in the form of a series of memorable learning experiences.

Mary Frances Claggett and Madge Holland
One or two semesters of elective "English by Individual Design" for juniors and seniors; discovery of self and relationships of self to society; problem-solving, inductive methods; flexible content.

Rationale and History — The humanities program at Alameda High School is in a constant state of flux. It may be helpful to think of it in terms of process, of becoming, rather than of being. To say that in one particular year we did such and such, is to say that and nothing more. A description of last year's syllabus would be invalid for this year and irrelevant for next year. It would be history.

To begin, then, with the history of the program — it began with students. We say that with emphasis and repeat, "It began with students who asked if we would talk to them about some books they had been reading. We would, and did, and the humanities forum, an amorphous but constant group, was formed." That group grew into an experimental summer school experience. And that group provided the impetus for initiating humanities courses into the curriculum, first as senior English alternatives, currently as electives in the junior-senior elective English program — "English by Individual Design." What began in 1963 as a small, extra-curricular group has evolved into a humanities program for 200 juniors and seniors each year.

Objectives — Objectives are usually formulated after the fact. These objectives, written after the fact and in educationalese, seem still to be valid:

1. To encourage a search for personal values through the study of creative thinkers in literature, art, science.
2. To provide an opportunity for students to develop a concept of the fully functioning individual.
3. To help students deal with problems of this generation by understanding creative thinkers of the past and present.
4. To encourage the development of an historical perspective in viewing the changing role of the individual in society.
5. To enable the student to define his concept of a fully functioning society by creating his own utopia.
6. To help students develop a problem-solving approach to learning.
7. To develop the creative potential of students by encouraging direct involvement in the arts.
8. To help students find increased pleasure and skill in writing, in listening, and in speaking.

Students — The most significant thing about our students is that they choose to be in the humanities program, which is open to all juniors and seniors as an English course that may be taken for one or both semesters. They are inventive, intelligent, and involved as well as demanding, difficult, and different each year. What was a successful book or activity one year may be a disaster the next.

Course of Study

> After it grew dark
> I began to want to change
> The way I grafted it.
> — Issa

Humanities I (one semester): Beginning with an inquiry into the nature of the fully functioning self, students explore various works of art and philosophy that focus on the discovery of the self and the relationship of the self to others.

Discussions stem from the reading of such works as: *Siddhartha, Oedipus, Hamlet, The Rhinoceros, Portrait of the Artist,* and *Science and Human Values.* Students engage in independent study and small group discussion; each student also completes one or more independent creative project. *Humanities II* (one semester): Humanities II, which may be taken independently from Humanities I, focuses on an investigation of the relationship of the individual to society. Each student tries to define his concept of utopia and its relevance to our present search for values. Class discussion proceeds from the reading of representative utopias and anti-utopias. In addition to reading widely from utopian literature, students carry on independent study in one aspect of society: education, social customs, government, and so forth. Each student also completes one or more creative projects during the semester.

Methods and Materials — The humanities courses have, from their inception, been taught by two English teachers who utilize the problem-solving, inductive method of teaching with large and small group discussions, individual and group research, and independent, sustained creative projects. Humanities films, art slides, records, and an extensive classroom library — provided initially by an NDEA grant — are available for student use. Field trips to plays, museums, and concerts give a cohesiveness to the group. Occasional guests — poets, musicians, speakers — contribute to the attempt to provide a variety of experiences for humanities students.

Activities and Resources — The San Francisco Bay area is extraordinarily rich in opportunities for participating in the current cultural scene. Students are increasingly involved in individual as well as group explorations into the artistic and socially-concerned life of the community.

Students frequently work together to make films or to study, for example, educational innovations in the area. They work independently on creative projects such as wood carving, pottery, painting, poetry, music, and dance. Once a week students and faculty gather at lunch to read their own poetry to the group. At the end of the school year, the humanities classes sponsor a school-wide festival of the arts.

Conclusions — Course descriptions usually sound good. They may sound too good and yet be dead. It is difficult to capture the essence of a course that is founded on the subtle shifts of interactions — between students, between students and teachers, between teachers — that gives the life spark to a program. The continuity is not in the books read, the assignments given, nor the projects completed. The continuity is the spirit that grows as a static classroom (no dividers, no carpet, no flexible scheduling) is transformed into a giant collage of sound and color that reflect each year humanities students who may say, as one did, "I am always free to be me in here."

Socrates A. Lagios*
Academically disinterested juniors and seniors; program based on values related to the themes "The Dignity of Man" and "Who Am I?" inductive, multi-media methods.

Rationale and Students — Our humanities program was offered to replace two required general English sections, one junior and one senior.

We feel the following characteristics describe our humanities student: He desires to learn but is aware that he is not developing the conceptual and symbolic notches in which to order his personal and vicarious experiences as he searches both himself and the world to discover how he can best face himself and society with purpose and direction.

In an educational culture espousing verbal intelligence, this student usually has verbal difficulties (especially reading); he also senses and feels most acutely an intellectual, social, and cultural gap widening between himself and his more academically successful classmates. Before this student takes the humanities program, he has gone through many changes: physical, social, emotional, and intellectual. Unfortunately, he is not usually able to synthesize these divergent changes into some framework or perspective. Poor study habits become firmly entrenched, and failure leads to disinterest in school. (Few would feel otherwise

---

* Mr. Lagios was involved in this humanities program from 1964 to 1967. He is presently the principal at J. W. Weeks Junior High School in Newton, Massachusetts.

if they knew only failure or near failure in most of their school experiences.) Generally he seeks outlets for his energy in other directions, mostly in non-school activities and occasionally in a fashion not condoned by society. There might also be an emotional barrier that deters him from realizing his full growth as a human being.

Although this student is not academically successful, he has an air of perpetual optimism (everything will turn out fine eventually); he has a canny wisdom and is quick to notice the tone of a statement; he likes immediate goals and rewards; long-range planning is not his forte (unless it is saving money to buy a car, a tangible reward); he is aware of his cultural shortcomings and wants to do something about them, but he is hesitant of leaving his peer group who afford him a sense of belonging.

The above characteristics are offered as a guideline. Although the class sections are homogeneous, there are many interesting individual traits within one group and a wide range of ability. Some have ability but appear to be lazy; others have minimal ability.

Approach — Our humanities program is based on values. These values are related to two basic themes, "The Dignity of Man" and "Who Am I?" The first theme and its subthemes focus on man generically, whereas the second basic theme calls attention to man as an individual. The following chart points out the themes and the various subject matter areas that can be included in the course. As the content and the method are interrelated, the student can go from the themes to the humanities or from the humanities to the themes, translating and interrelating the world of everyday life and the world of imagination. In essence, the student does his own learning at his own pace in what might be termed an inductive approach. (Students also learn affectively, which sometimes does not include a logical development.)

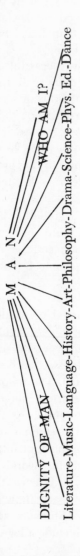

DIGNITY OF MAN

Literature-Music-Language-History-Art-Philosophy-Drama-Science-Phys. Ed.-Dance

WHO AM I?

M A N

Civic Responsibilities
Universal Values
Individual's Conflict with
     Himself
Developing a Personal
     Philosophy

Family of Man
Man and His Work
Man and His Leisure

Man's Concern for Others

BECAUSE.   BECAUSE I. . . .

Man as a Victim
Man in Survival
Man's Need for Adventure
Man's Hopes
Man's Pride

Materials and Content — The chart is placed on the front blackboard in the classroom, and learning is inductive as each student makes his own evaluations and justifies them on the basis of the content being considered. Quite often comments follow a circular pattern, going from student to chart to another student, with the teacher playing a secondary role. This tack, plus the use of many media — books, films, records, plastic materials, guest lecturers, and field trips — enable the student to bring into play more of his senses in learning rather than just focusing on the printed word. The Gestalt approach seems to have distinct advantages for the student as he learns.

The "Because." and "Because I. . . ." in the chart are vital. The "Because." says to the student that he can have an opinion or an idea and not be able to express it fully, but he would get credit for trying, whether orally or in any other kind of exercise. In essence we feel students want to learn — in three years, only one student used "Because." and only once at that. The "Because I. . . ." shows a fuller development in the student's ability to express his ideas and feelings.

Of all the media used, the students, based on their yearly evaluation of the program and their daily comments, felt that they learned more from viewing films than from any other technique. I would agree with their observation. There are no slow learners in viewing films. All go through the experience at the same time. About the film *On the Waterfront*, a student said that Terry was cleansed when he fell into the river and he had to make the walk up to the gang leader by himself. Another student felt that Terry and Mountain in *Requiem for a Heavyweight* were alike because in choosing to become free, they both had to suffer.

Here is an example of how a number of media are interrelated. While reading *Hiroshima* by John Hersey, the students viewed a film about the lead plane on the flight. They also listened to the ideas of a scientist who spoke on the role of research and the conflicts therein. Almost any activity lends itself to this technique, but there has to be some preplanning. Flexibility comes in letting the students do the learning, and at times encouraging them to plan some of the activities.

Evaluation — An evaluation chart is given to each student twice a term and the teacher and student go over it together. The student's yearly evaluation appears to be very helpful. Another possible technique is for the student to evaluate himself independently of the teacher and then for the two of them to go over it together.

Richard F. North
"The Interpretation of Experience"; interdisciplinary under English department; junior and senior elective; objective and subjective consideration of man, self, and creativity.

Rationale — At Byram Hills High School we consider humanities an approach to gaining insights into man's interpretation of experience as well as the direct experience itself. In fact, if there were a name given to the course other than humanities, it would be "The Interpretation of Experience."

Within the framework of experience and the interpretation of it, the basic methodology is metaphor or comparison. Since, as learning theorists point out, we know nothing except in relation to something else, then the mind is a kind of metaphor where experience is integrated and interpreted in the light of other experiences. In other words, since people learn through comparison, we teach comparatively. This may be better understood from the following examples dealing with the concept of time and its various subdivisions:

Time in physics: the theory of relativity
Time in painting: the depiction of time in surrealism
Time in literature: the stream-of-consciousness novel
Time in music
Time in language: tense and the linguistic relativity hypothesis
Time and psychology: time as a dimension of consciousness
Sociological concepts of time
Time and history

Basically what we do is compare and contrast these subdivisions with the hope that students will be better equipped to differentiate experiences for themselves.

The implication of the above is that humanities at Byram Hills High School is an interdisciplinary course with an emphasis on a comparison and analysis of related experiences.

Objectives

1. To draw from a variety of different disciplines to illustrate that history, literature, language, religion, psychology, the arts, and so on, all have elements in common and are not disparate studies to be considered exclusive of one another. That is, there exists, in some sense, a common essence that is applicable to all. This is so, even if we only consider the creative urge that has given them birth.

2. To show students that in the midst of specialization and fragmentation there is a totality or wholeness to man — that man is in a constant state of process and contingency.

3. To illustrate how the two polarities of human experience — objectivity and subjectivity — are inextricably interwoven and that identification and internalization of both are necessary for an understanding of the whole experience and the pragmatic uses that knowledge of this polarity will bring. An example is decision-making.

4. To define and discuss the role played by reason, logic, sensitivity, and intuition in man's evolution.

5. To define and discuss the nature of the concept "value."

6. To emphasize humanities as a means and not an end to knowledge.

7. To encourage students to take part in creating curricula.

8. To encourage students' direct experience in the creation of their own artistic projects.

9. To de-emphasize the importance of grades.

10. To feel no great compulsion to finish the course.

Students and Staff — The course, under the administration of the English department, is an elective and meets three times a week for one year. It is taught by one teacher and various specialists when necessary and available. The students participating in the course comprise about 20 per cent of the high school student body and are a heterogeneous, yet high level, group of about 70 boys and girls, most of whom are juniors and seniors.

Course Requirements

1. One research paper of about 17 typewritten pages, the topic of which may be anything providing it meets the requirements of the senior thesis that all students must complete upon graduation. Leeway is allowed regarding the student's own point of view and creative insight. An advisor to oversee the writing of the paper is optional.

2. In lieu of the research paper, the student is encouraged to experiment and create original work in other mediums such as painting, sculpture, or music. An advisor is required.

3. During the year there are at least five reaction papers of about two to five typewritten pages in length. These papers are used to assess reactions to and comprehension of lectures and group activities. They are also used as departure points for discussion, which may or may not be directly associated with the given topic or lecture.

4. Each student is expected to do at least one oral report on any topic of his choice. Generally the report is a brief explication of his research project.

5. Examinations are of the take-home variety with the intention of evaluating the student on what he knows rather than on what he does not know. A mid-term, for example, would be comprised of seven questions to be studied, two of which would be assigned in class.

6. At the end of the year the student is asked to write an evaluation of the course and the personnel involved.

Course of Study — Inasmuch as the basic objective of the course is to discuss and evaluate different kinds of human experiences and man's interpretation of them, at the onset students are given material written by the staff indicating the variety of experiences man has. The student is then asked to evaluate the experiences, and he invariably comes up with two different kinds — rational and irrational. He is then introduced to the concepts of objectivity and subjectivity. There follows a cursory, but not necessarily brief, discussion of the questions implied by this dichotomy. The intention of these discussions is to introduce the three general areas of inquiry the student will be dealing with — man, self, and creativity.

Because of student involvement in creating curriculum, there sometimes occur topics that do not reflect in a meaningful way any of the above or cannot be dealt with in a sophisticated manner either by the staff or by the students. However, there is relatively little that comes up that is not applicable to the above areas and that, with a little compromise and insight, cannot be made contemporary and relevant to most students. In any case, the only stipulations of the course are that (1) students deal with the two basic approaches to interpreting experience and that (2) we begin with an objective or scientific view of man to develop a few working definitions. The obvious beginning then is physical and cultural anthropology.

Following is a brief outline of this area of the course:

I. Anthropology — Man
  A. The emphasis here is on LaBarre's *The Human Animal.* Discussion covers the following areas: primates, hand, eye, brain complex, sexuality and the origins of family and marriage, language, human character and morality, and their relation to biology and the ultimate question, "What does it mean to be human?"
  B. *Patterns of Culture* discusses two basic kinds of cultures: the Appollonian and the Dionysian. This di-

chotomy is similar to the objective and subjective polarity and emphasizes "primitive" man's interpretation of experience.

C. At this point, there is a series of lectures and discussions emanating from material written by the staff on the corollary subjects of religion and "primitive" religion as well as Meerloo's *Rape of the Mind*. Subjects discussed are: the origin and nature of religion, common factors in primitive religions, child psychology and primitive religion, and the psychology of the totalitarian state.

D. Readings: Ruth Benedict. *Patterns of Culture*. Boston: Houghton Mifflin Co., 1934, and Weston LaBarre. *The Human Animal*. Chicago: Phoenix Books, 1955.

As is obvious, the emphasis moves from an observation of man's external activities to an observation of his internal activities, that is, his psychology. In all of the above areas, the subjective and objective dichotomy in human experience is discussed at length. The following outline describes the second part of the elective, which is basically lecture-discussion written by the staff.

II. Psychology and Religion — The Self

A. As an interesting aside, preliminary discussion centers around the subject of parapsychology. Topics discussed are: subjective experience and ESP, physics, causality and the interpretation of phenomena, and the Psi experience and religion.

B. From the above discussion, it becomes obvious to the student that the central question is, "What is this thing that interprets experience?" Areas emphasized are: learning theory, the nature of thought, reason, logic, and intuition, the dimensions of consciousness, non-verbal behavior, symbolization, dream, myth, the drug experience versus the religious experience, the creative experience and art, and the nature of the self.

C. Related to the above discussion is the place of science and religion in interpreting man's experience as well as discovering why he interprets as he does. Again the basic dichotomy is obviously the objective arm of science and the subjective arm of religion. Topics discussed here are: the controversy between science and religion, the kinds of reality or truth both represent, the scientific self and the religious self, science and religion as systems of inquiry and explanation, the descriptive versus the prescriptive, the effect of technology on the psychology of contemporary man, and the death of God movement and Martin Buber's concept of I and Thou.

D. Because Western man is so positive of his existence and that he has a self, discussion turns to those who have a different view of the self. Areas considered here are: introductory material on the history of India and the development of Hinduism, the concepts of karma, atman, paramatman and moksa, introductory material on the development of Buddhism, Buddha, karma and the Four Noble Truths, nirvana and the negation of self, Zen Buddhism, and the koan and satori. The very different interpretations of the Hindu and Buddhist regarding self is obvious here.

E. Readings: William Barrett. *Irrational Man*. New York: Anchor Books, 1962; Will Durant. *The Story of Philosophy*. New York: Clarion Books, 1967; Sigmund Freud. *Civilization and Its Discontents*. New York: W. W. Norton, 1961; Erich Fromm. *The Forgotten Language*. New York: Grove Press, 1951; Aldous Huxley. *The Doors of Perception*. New York: Harper Colophon, 1963; Eric and Mary Josephson, eds. *Man Alone*. New York: Dell Pub. Co., 1962; Carl Jung. *Modern Man in Search of a Soul*. New York: Harcourt, Brace, 1933; Susanne Langer. *Philosophy in a New Key*. New York: Mentor Books, 1951; Joost Meerloo. *The Rape of the*

Mind. New York: Universal Library, 1956; J. B. Rhine. *New World of the Mind.* New York: Vintage, 1953; and Alan Watts. *The Joyous Cosmology.* New York: Vintage, 1962.

With the close of this second and most rigorous part of the course, students proceed to use the tools they have acquired during the year by discussing as many of the literary readings as time allows. The purpose is to involve students more deeply in the aesthetic experience and also encourage the direct creative experience itself through the artist's own projects. Wherever possible, students' works are critiqued as well as the works of established composers and artists.

III. Interpretation and the Creative Experience
   A. The emphasis here is on an author's interpretation of experience, his characters' interpretation of experience, the reader's interpretation of the work as a whole, the kinds of thinking and aesthetic processes involved in the writer's creation of the work as well as the reader's appreciation of it, the philosophical questions raised by the work, and the work's relevance to the student and the course.
   B. Readings: Andre Gide. *Strait is the Gate.* New York: Vintage Books, 1952; Nikos Kazantzakis. *Report to Greco.* New York: Bantam Books, 1965; ———. *Zorba the Greek.* New York: Simon and Schuster, 1952; J. D. Salinger. *Franny and Zooey.* New York: Bantam Books, 1961; and various essays and works of poetry.

Eugene Fairbanks
Elective for juniors and seniors; separate humanities department; team-teaching; interdisciplinary; informal atmosphere, creativity, and participation encouraged.

Approach and Objectives — The focus is upon enjoyment and appreciation of the arts, the growth of questioning minds, and a philosophic attitude toward the meaning of life, self-identity, human solidarity, and aesthetic and ethical values. Therefore, the course concerns itself very little with technical matters. The primary concern is with man's being rather than his doing.

Students verbalize their appreciation, agreement, and disagreement, and the class, including instructors, sit in a circle so that dialogue can be carried on face to face. An attempt is made to keep the atmosphere of the class as informal and uninhibited as possible.

The original goal was to develop a humanities program based on discussion rather than lecture. The year begins by asking the students to identify themselves not only by name but also by their beliefs and convictions. The instructors identify themselves in much the same way. This helps to free students somewhat from an inhibited response to our questions.

The humanities has been offered as a course of study for four years in the Wappingers Central School System. It is felt that a humanities course should emphasize the relationship between the arts, social sciences, and, to a certain extent, the nature sciences and their dependence on one another as means of expressing the human condition. No humanities course can exclude historical and philosophical perspectives, nor can it perpetuate the pigeonholing of the arts as separate, technically different disciplines.

Students and Requirements — The course is open to all juniors and seniors as an elective course. A team of three teachers meets each day with the class. The humanities department is a separate and independent department that works closely with other departments in the school.

The word "requirement" has been eliminated from the program. Student involvement is encouraged, as is research, performing, and class presentations by individuals and groups. A humanities night is offered, and original plays, poems, films, and music are performed by the students. An extensive bibliography is offered to the students.

Content — The course content is open to change and modification as students and teachers see the need for change. There are six units of study in the course outline.

I. Exploration of artists' reactions to topical issues of their times.
   A. Music: songs of protest (prejudice, etc.), work songs, war songs, current problem songs, Britten's *War Requiem*, Shostakovitch's Symphony #13, and Tchaikovsky's *Romeo & Juliet* and *1812 Overture*
   B. Art: evolution of *Guernica*, slides of social commentary (Kollwitz, Rivera, Shahn, etc.), slides of satirical comment (Daumier, Goya, Rowlandson, Gropper, etc.) and Coventry Cathedral (new and old)
   C. Literature
      1. Poetry: Wilfred Owen's from *The War Requiem*, Archibald MacLeish's *Frescoes for Mr. Rockefeller's City* (6 panels), and miscellaneous war poetry and poetry of social protest
      2. Selections from: Orwell's *Homage to Catalonia*, Remarque's *All Quiet on the Western Front*, Agee's *Let Us Now Praise Famous Men*, Steinbeck's *The Grapes*

of Wrath, Thurber's *The Last Flower,* St. Exupery's *Wind, Sand, and Stars,* March's *Company K,* Romain's *Verdun,* and Bierce's *In the Midst of Life*

3. Films: *Harvest of Shame,* I and II, and *War in Spain*

II. Mythology and the Bible as they relate to man's understanding of himself and his relationship to the physical and metaphysical. It begins with a discussion of primitive art and magic and moves toward mythology, concentrating on three or four basic myths as tentative answers to some basic universal problems that have puzzled man over the centuries.

A. Music: *Missa Luba,* Stravinsky's *Oedipus Rex,* selection of Psalms, Verdi's *Manzoni Requiem,* an American jazz mass, selection of spirituals, selection of Gregorian chants, and Tchaikowsky's *Francesca Da Rimini*

B. Art: slides of Greek and non-Greek gods, slides of mythological heroes, slides of Tympanum sculpture, slides of the Sistine Chapel and *Last Judgment,* slides of Dore's illustrations for Dante, and slides of William Blake's illustrations

C. Literature: Dante's *Inferno,* Sophocles' *Oedipus Rex,* myths (Venus, Narcissus, Orpheus), *King James Bible* (Job), MacLeish's *JB,* Johnson's *God's Trombones* (4 selections), and Shaw's *Don Juan in Hell*

III. One author, one painter, and one composer are discussed in depth to make students aware of the relationship between an artist's life and his work. The approach is biographical, social, psychological, historical, and aesthetic. We try to choose works that lend themselves to this approach. The artists chosen did not lead exemplary lives, but their contribution to man have been outstanding. They are interesting because their lives were tragic and self-defeating.

A. Musician — Tchaikowsky: life, musical characteristics, compositions, Symphony #5 in E Minor, and Piano Concerto #1 in B^b Minor (see also I, A and II, A).

B. Painter: life and slides used in conjunction with biographical sketch to show his development

C. Writer — Dylan Thomas: poetry and essays to illustrate his attitudes toward love, birth, death, life, religion, and to his craft, selections for Brinnin's biography and Caitlin Thomas's autobiography, Dame Edith Sitwell's tribute, and *Under Milkwood*

IV. Exploration of the artist's function to represent the world and people as he sees them, to unify experiences, and to strengthen the experience through a strong appeal to the senses. We study experiences that are ugly or evil in a variety of ways: the tragic, the pathetic, the comic, and a combination of all three — the tragicomic.

A. Music: Moussorgsky's *A Night on Bald Mountain,* Bizet's *Carmen,* and Orff's *Carmina Burana*

B. Art: Henri de Toulouse Lautrec, James Ensor, Edvard Munch, Hieronymus Bosch, Surrealism, and Tchelitchew's *Hide and Seek*

C. Literature: Miller's *Death of a Salesman* (tragedy and the pathetic), O'Casey's *Juno and the Paycock* (tragicomedy), Wilde's *The Importance of Being Earnest,* and miscellaneous poetry and prose

V. Style is traced through several periods of art pointing out the historical-geographical categories of style. Groups, schools, or individuals whose characteristics are so distinctive that they become a sub-type are also studied.

A. Historical

B. National or geographic

C. Schools or groups

D. Individual

E. Attitudinal: Classic, romantic, tragic, and comic

F. Characteristics of each style influenced by: medium, philosophy, technique, and organization

G. Music: baroque, classical, romantic, impressionistic, and contemporary

H. Sculpture: Egyptian, Greek, Renaissance, impression-istic, and modern
I. Literature: neo-classical, romantic, Victorian, and modern
VI. The various levels of value in art from the merely pretty or graceful to the beautiful and sublime are studied.
  A. Subjective relativism — standard of taste
  B. Objective absolutism: standards of artistic quality, artistic integrity, artistic truth, and artistic greatness (depth, breadth, and inexhaustibility)
  C. Comparison of works with same theme or subject
  D. Comparison of the three disciplines treatment of the same theme or subject
  E. Analysis of a single work in depth

Materials and Resources — The school system has an excellent resource library where hundreds of slides, records, 2D and 3D reproductions, and magazines are available. Films are also available through the audio-visual department.

Thomas H. McMullen
Humanities department incorporating English, social studies, and fine arts departments; four 25-minute modules daily for juniors and seniors; team-teaching; three tracks; student curriculum advisors.

Rationale — Del Norte opened its doors in 1964 with a commitment to innovation, not for the sake of change alone, but change in the direction of providing a curriculum more relevant to today's student than that offered by traditional concepts. The major emphasis of the program has been to break down the heretofore accepted idea that subject matter is isolated and distinct and to create a learning situation that shows subject matter is not fragmented but very definitely related. In keeping with this philosophy, the humanities department, which encompasses the English, social studies, and fine arts departments, was created, with a chairman to correlate and coordinate activities within these areas and to provide liaison with other departments in the school.

In developing a definition of purpose or *raison d'etre*, Del Norte tried always to keep the students in mind.

Objectives — Humanities is the inquiry into the interrelationship of those aspects of cultural development that provide the individual with a consciousness of his role in the culture. Understanding of this role is accomplished through exposure to the traditions of the past, involvement in the cultural forces of the present, and interpretation of new directions as they will shape the complex society of the future. Within this ideal, the objectives are condensed into three:

1. To promote understanding and to cultivate awareness of the factors that have shaped the society in which we live — social forces, writings, thought, the arts, and the sciences.
2. To develop insights into the concepts of our civilization and its institutions — political, economic, religious, social, and cultural.
3. To provide consciousness of new directions within these institutions as they react together and to aid the student to define his role within that structure.

Approach and Structure — To meet the needs set forth in the curricular objectives, the traditionally required courses at the junior and senior levels were combined as follows:

GRADE	REQUIRED SUBJECTS	NEW DESIGNATION
11	U. S. history English III	Junior humanities
12	World history English IV	Senior humanities

Students are assigned to teams composed of four teachers (two English and two history) for four modules daily (modules are of 25 minute duration.) The teams, assisted by the music and art teachers who serve as consultants and develop special programs for and with students, evolve their own schedule, organizing large group presentations, small group activities, and individual conferences. The student-teacher ratio is approximately 30 to one, and there are three tracks: college preparatory, technical-vocational, and developmental. Teams are permitted wide latitude in arranging course content, program, and schedules. It should also be emphasized that student advisory groups in each team are included in the planning and development and often in the conduct of the classes.

Courses of Study

Junior humanities: This combines the traditional U. S. history and English III courses. It is built around the theme, "What It Means to Be an American." Beyond the basic core of material, which includes the study of the great documents, research techniques for the college bound, practical composition, major political and literary figures, governmental processes, folk art, and music, the students are afforded opportunity for in-depth studies of their personal interest in such areas as the American novel, creative expression, the United Nations, the nature of dissent, and poetry. The nature of enrichment depends upon student interest and varies from team to team.

Senior humanities: This utilizes the basic framework of the world history and English IV courses and concentrates upon the traditions of the past as they relate to the world in which we live. The essentials here include the foundations of democracy, establishment of aesthetic principles, the nature of renaissance in the creative arts, composition, comparative literature, practical consumer economics, and the great writers. In-depth studies include such varied areas as the Reformation, expansionism, Africa, Shakespeare, reading for enjoyment and information, business correspondence, and art of the 20th century. Again student advisory groups assist the teams in developing the type of program to be offered.

Each course requires that the students master the minimum essentials within the structure of that course, and they are permitted as much freedom as possible in meeting their own capabilities.

Needless to say, the developmental humanities requires a great deal more structuring so that the elective aspects are somewhat minimal, while the college preparatory program may rely more heavily upon enrichment. The technical-vocational attempts to provide a happy medium in practical application for the students who will end their formal education with the high school diploma.

Materials and Resources — Within the limits of the financial resources, as wide a variety of materials and resources as possible are utilized. These are enhanced by a separate humanities resource center containing books, records, filmstrips, and study packets as well as student purchases of special paperbacks and resources (although these are kept to a minimum.)

There is no formal syllabus since Del Norte is presently refining, adapting, and modifying its program to more adequately meet the needs of each student in his goal of self-discovery. Though this is a continuing process, it is anticipated that a somewhat definitive syllabus will be forthcoming within the next two to three years.

Joe Baxley
Examines human values through artistic and philosophical activities; senior elective; independent and small group study and participation; multi-media resources.

Objectives

1. To involve students in an examination of human values.
2. To encourage students to express their ideas, measuring them against those of past and present philosophers and artists.
3. To expose students to some philosophers of the past, relating them to the present.
4. To examine those aspects of the arts that are non-verbal.
5. To show philosophy and the arts as reflections of individual and collective man in a particular environment.
6. To encourage students to express their ideas in the forms examined in the course, both verbal and non-verbal.

Approach — Although a chronological approach is used, this is not a survey course. The main objective is to involve the students in philosophical and artistic activities called humanities. It is believed that through this involvement, the student will become more familiar with himself and develop more understanding of his fellow man. Humanities is defined as the ideas of man and his methods of expressing them. Philosophy, including methodology, ethics, aesthetics, and metaphysics, gives the ideas; the arts, literature, painting, drawing and related media, sculpture, dance, music, and architecture are the means of expression. The basic individual differences and similarities are studied so that the student has some idea of methods of verbal and non-verbal communication. Beginning with the Greeks of the Golden Age, the fundamentals are introduced both in philosophy and the arts.

The second area of study, the Middle Ages, is examined as a continuation of philosophy and the arts as influenced by a specific institution. The Renaissance reveals the process of reusing the past within the context of a new age. These three periods are covered in the first term, yet students continue relating to the present by means of universal concepts. During the second half of the year the subject matter consists of contemporary philosophy and the arts. The wealth of material allows for individual study and presentations to the class, with emphasis on individual discovery and development.

Students and Staff — The course is open to any senior and is taught by one instructor. A full-year course is offered, meeting five periods per week.

Requirements — Only because grades are part of the system are they used; they are arrived at by means of a contract system. Specific requirements are established at the beginning of each marking term. Great latitude is allowed for individual interest. For example, for a student to receive a grade of A, he writes an informal paper of 750 words, attends two musical and/or dramatic performances, watches four hours of TV, does an art project, and reads 100 pages of collateral reading. Nine weeks is the marking term for these requirements. Short oral and/or written reports dealing with content and evaluation are prepared.

Materials — All students read *Plato's Dialogues,* Washington Square Press edition. The remainder of the reading is done on an individual or small group basis, with teacher approval, and oral reports and discussion. If students wish to read a work as a class, this may be done. Slides are used to illustrate art of the past; also local art museums are visited. TV is used when appropriate programs are offered. Rather than a required list of reading or a rigid selection of pictures or music, an attempt is made to use material that seems to be relevant to the directions taken by the students.

Resources and Activities — Members of the community involved in philosophy and the arts are used both as consultants and instructors. Any teachers who have interest in the humanities are used when possible.

Students are encouraged to become involved in both individual and group art activities. Some have found new interest in areas that they had never explored, much less participated in. The art projects offer this opportunity. These projects are not graded but are shown and discussed as experiments, not masterpieces. Students are encouraged to visit art museums in the area and try their own criticism, using the fundamental information given at the beginning of the course.

Richard Kamka
Emphasizes first-hand experiences with arts; films are heart of course; senior elective; team-teaching; flexible, changing content.

Rationale and Approach — During the first semester, Humanities 12 offers experience with cinema, photography, painting, collage, construction, sculpture, and environment; architecture, music (classical, rock, blues, folk, jazz, etc.), dance, drama, musical comedy, and opera are offered the second semester. Various relationships between the art forms provide transitions, but even these relationships do not become the course's content. Our approach, neither historical, thematic, nor philosophic, de-emphasizes content in order to provide first-hand experiences with art. Our approach is aesthetic with emphasis on ". . . observation of the arts and the kinds of human activity they involve. . . . The primary aim is to guide the student in arriving inductively at a few broad principles and concepts which are applicable to . . . art creations." [1]

Materials

The Humanities: Applied Aesthetics, 4th ed. Dudley, Louise, and Faricy, Austin. New York: McGraw-Hill, 1967.

The Medium Is the Message. McLuhan, Marshall, and Fiore, Quentin. New York: Random House, 1967. Only these books are required reading; all other books are suggested on an individual basis.

Supplementary and reserve room libraries

---

1. Dudley, Louise, and Faricy, Austin. *The Humanities: Applied Aesthetics,* 4th ed. New York: McGraw-Hill, 1967.

Films — the heart of the course.

Recordings

Field trips to: Art Institute, Contemporary Art Museum, art galleries, Illinois Institute of Technology campus, University of Chicago campus, Chicago Loop architecture, Frank Lloyd Wright Oak Park architecture, The Auditorium — dance performance, Harper Theatre — dance performance, Orchestra Hall, Opera House, and Studebaker Theatre

Paintings, sculptures, photographs, and so on borrowed from students, teachers, and local artists

Guests artists from the local area

Television: Each Monday students received a schedule of TV programs for the week.

Instructors and Students — The demands that Humanities 12 places upon a teacher's knowledge and experience make necessary the team-teaching approach. The teachers should be enthusiastic to the degree that they are part-time artists and aware of their contemporaries.

As an elective, Humanities 12 is open to any senior regardless of IQ scores, reading scores, or grade point average. Neither counselor approval nor former teacher recommendation but only student willingness and formal registration are needed to take the course for credit. The course is designed to serve the student whose experience with the various contemporary art forms has been limited and who is anxious for such experience.

Requirements — Homework consists almost entirely of keeping a journal in which the student records his experiences with the arts or other aesthetic experiences he may have. The journal, referred to as the "listening, observing, reading log," is read by the teacher every three or four weeks and accounts for at least one-half of a student's final grade each marking period.

Course of Study — The course of study is brief. It must not be considered binding. Relying as it does on so many audio-visual aids,[2] field trips, and guests, the course of study must remain flexible and ready to take advantage of materials when opportunities for them present themselves. Flexibility is also very important to permit for response to student needs and to allow for spontaneity that can encourage student and teacher enthusiasm and creativity.

Three sample outlines for the course of study follow:

I. Introduction to Humanities 12, approximately three weeks
   A. The medium
   B. The senses
   C. The artist: black humor, irony, satire, fraud, "the put on," and "the come on"
   D. the audience: tolerance, "the fake-out," "the cop-out," and "camp"
   E. Art

---

2. NOTE: Because the York High School program relies so heavily upon film and because film annotations have been omitted from course descriptions, the following list may be useful to humanities instructors: *An Occurrence at Owl Creek Bridge, Artists: Andy Warhol and Roy Lichtenstein, Artists: Claes Oldenburg, Artists: Frank Stella and Larry Poons: The New Abstraction, Artists: Jack Tworkov, Artists: Jasper Johns, Artists: Jim Dine, Artists: Robert Rauschenberg, Art of Marie Cosindas, Chicago Picasso, Choreographer at Work, Colors in Music, Composers: Electronic Music, Dance: Anna Sokolow's "Rooms," Dance: Echoes of Jazz, Dance: Four Pioneers, Dance: In Search of "Lovers," Discovering Color, Discovering Composition in Art, Discovering Creative Pattern, Discovering Dark and Light, Discovering Form in Art, Discovering Harmony in Art, Discovering Ideas for Art, Discovering Line, Discovering Perspective, Discovering Texture, Dream of the Wild Horses, Editing Synchronous Sound, Everybody's Dreamhouse, Film Problems, Film Splicing with Griswold and Harwaid Splicers, Giacometti, The Hand, Language of the Camera Eye, Language of Dance, Meaning in Modern Painting, parts 1 and 2, Meter and Rhythm, The Mime, Modern Music, Music and Emotion, Music Makers of the Blue Ridge, Music as Sound, Nature of Clay, Nothing Happened This Morning, Photography: Dorothea Lange: The Closer for Me, Poetry: Allen Ginsberg and Lawrence Ferlinghetti, Religion, The Stage Evolves, Stravinsky, Technique, Time Is, Touch Clay, A Ceramic Experience, Voices of the String Quartet, What Will You Tear Down Next? Writers: Bruce Jay Friedman and Black Humor,* and *Writers: John Updike.*

110

II. Cinema, approximately four weeks
  A. The medium
    1. Types: features, documentaries, experimentals, underground, instructional, and shorts
    2. Animation
    3. Composition
    4. Rhythm
    5. Time
    6. Nuance
    7. Motion
    8. Sound
III. Photography, approximately three weeks
  A. The medium
    1. Types: portraiture, architectural, documentary, and art
    2. Composition
    3. Space
    4. Nuance
    5. Texture
    6. Line
    7. Rhythm

Other units include:
IV. Painting, approximately five weeks
V. Collage, construction, and environmentalism, approximately one week
VI. Sculpture, approximately two weeks
VII. Architecture, approximately two weeks
VIII. Music, approximately five weeks
IX. Poetry and music, approximately one week
X. Dance, approximately four weeks
XI. Drama, approximately three weeks
XII. Opera and musical comedy, approximately three weeks: This unit draws heavily on the preceding units of music, poetry, dance, and drama.

Carl Ladensack

Stresses that arts are related and are expressions of man's awareness of life; junior and senior full-year elective (except for those with reading difficulties); team-teachers and guests; discussion encouraged; individual projects in art, literature, music, and drama.

Objectives — Currently under revision, the Scarsdale High School humanities program has operated for seven years. During that time its objectives have periodically increased and shifted emphasis as student needs and interests have differed, but generally it has attempted to achieve some standard goals:

1. To bring to students a realization that arts are not peripheral to man's concern but are expressions of his deepest awareness.
2. To show that all arts relate and that each is merely an expression in a different medium in accordance with the individual artist's personality and area of competence.
3. To alert the student to the analogous content of various arts.
4. To discover *how* arts mean so that the student will be free to seek for himself additional insights.
5. To allow the students to honor and evaluate all forms of expression rather than a limited number, i.e., the dancer may speak as clearly as the writer to those prepared to comprehend his statement.
6. To stress an interest in living rather than skills for earning a living.

Approach — The course is designed to teach general concepts instead of any particular views or attitudes. Primarily it is a search for patterns in ideas, form, style, function, and quality that cross disciplinary lines. For example, although it may seem simplistic, the emphasis is on noting such matters as the beginning, middle, and end of an artifact to show that art differs from life because the artist gives experience to a work that heightens awareness.

Students and Instructors — The course is an elective open to juniors and seniors. Originally students who lacked maturity and a sense of responsibility were eliminated since the course was partly an experiment in extending privileges to students. At present the total student body enjoys the freedom that was extended to the first class. Now only those with reading difficulties that would prevent their handling the course material are excluded. (These students could be included in a humanities course with different content.)

The major portion of the course is taught by a team of three or four teachers from different disciplines (art, literature, music, and drama). The team's work is supplemented by guest appearances of members of the community and students with special competence.

Requirements — Within the course there is no stress on papers or tests. Some written assignments are even optional. We emphasize experience and analysis of its significance. Since in the non-academic world people seldom write papers about books that they have read or films they have seen, we try to avoid that response and stress the more normal activity — discussion. Skills and drills remain the province of the individual disciplines.

The course meets four days a week for 52 minutes each time, lasts a full year, and carries one full credit.

Activities — One of the strong elements of the course has been the individual projects that students may conduct independently or with the aid of a mentor. Many have proven distinctive and genuinely educational. Each student is urged to work in the area of his greatest interest and competence and to let the project take any appropriate form. Thus students may compose, paint, sculpt, construct, write, conduct research, photograph, record, or perform in other ways. Many of these projects are presented to the class or placed on display where the entire school may see them. We urge students to plan an activity early in the year and to work at it throughout the term. Since students are no more responsible than the rest of us and work best when there is a deadline, we try to have periodic progress reports.

Resources and Materials — We use the community as much as possible and the art and architecture of Yale University as well as the galleries and museums of New York City.

During the summer prior to the course, students read Sigmund Freud's *Civilization and Its Discontents,* C. G. Jung's *Modern Man in Search of a Soul,* and Sir James Frazer's *Golden Bough.* During the school year the reading includes Franz Kafka's *Metamorphosis,* William Faulkner's *Light in August,* Albert Camus' *Stranger,* Virgil's *Aeneid,* Henrik Ibsen's *Rosmersholm* and *The Master Builder,* Joseph Machlis' *Enjoyment of Music,* Sarah Newmeyer's *Enjoying Modern Art,* and selected poetry by Wallace Stevens, Hart Crane, T. S. Eliot, William Carlos Williams, William Butler Yeats, Gerard Manley Hopkins, Dylan Thomas and others.

We use a few films such as Encyclopedia Britannica's *What Is a Painting?* and *Chartres Cathedral,* and a Museum of Modern Art film called *N.Y., N.Y.* Our record and slide collections contain works from all ages, styles, and schools.

Helen H. Winn

Anthropological and philosophical focus; required of all seniors; separate humanities department but works closely with English department; multi-media; team-teaching and guests; large and small group instruction; individual creative projects.

Rationale — The proliferation of humanities programs in American education is a source of hope to those concerned about the relevance of traditional courses of study in today's world. Good or bad, these new programs represent an attempt to meet a perceived need and to correct a present educational deficiency.

While political history has long been a staple of the American public school curriculum, it is becoming apparent to many that basic insights into the root causes of cultural variations and the human motivations that lie behind events are increasingly lost in an endless effort to cope with the accumulation of factual information. Knowledge about human behavior patterns, given new impetus by the relatively young disciplines of psychology, anthropology, and archaeology, has led many of us engaged in secondary school teaching to question the traditional curricular patterns that were effective a generation ago but seem surprisingly insular in today's shrunken world. Information about the great ideas of man, the philosophy, religion, art, architecture, and music of people not only in Europe and America, but also in Asia, Africa, and South America, is not available to the average high school student in any coherent or regular way. A narrow education in the conventions developed by our own culture will not help us to understand, for instance, the ancient and very real differences that characterize peoples of the emerging Asian and African nations.

Furthermore, the emphasis on science and mathematics, which admittedly cannot be neglected within today's realities, has tended to mitigate against humanistic studies. The most dangerous thing a civilization can do, however, is to develop highly trained specialists, scientists, and technicians who are not equally equipped with insight into the workings of men's minds and the forces of society.

The humanities course developed at the River Dell Senior High School is based on a belief that a clear need exists for re-emphasis on human values and human understanding in today's technology-oriented society and that schools should at least try to meet this need. We believe that such a course may help to solve a growing problem in American education that, in its effort to cope with the knowledge explosion, all too often loses sight of the meaning behind facts.

Objectives — The River Dell humanities course attempts to consider the growth and development of such universal and basic ideas as law, religion, morality, government, and man's place in the universe and to account for the wide variety of forms these ideas have taken in a number of different cultures. A major goal of the program is to increase student understanding of our own society and time through an examination of man's basic needs, the institutions through which he endeavors to meet his needs, and the role of the artist and the arts in interpreting the social condition.

Such a course at the high school level is not intended as a terminus for our students. Rather, its purpose is to give direction to their thinking, provide a *modus operandi* for evaluating the bewildering modern world, and to whet appetites for more information. Our primary goal in offering the humanities course is to induce a humanistic sensitivity in our students and to stimulate them to read, look, listen, and think in other than mechanistic ways as they mature.

Students — The River Dell humanities course is of sufficient rigor to require a degree of maturity on the part of its participants. For this reason it is given to our most mature students, the seniors, who are at the culmination of their public school experience and on the verge of adulthood.

It is the philosophy of the program that a humanities course has value for students of all levels of ability. Accordingly, the program is required of all seniors rather than offered as an elective to an elite few. Differences in ability and level of preparation are accommodated within the individual classroom; the readings are appropriately modified for the slower student.

The course replaces English as a major requirement in the senior year; a revision of the English curriculum has been made, however, to retain the former senior year's content through consolidation of the whole English curriculum and re-evaluation of the generally unsatisfactory tenth year literature program. The humanities department is separate and independent but works closely with other humanities areas and with English in particular so that the two subjects complement and support each other.

Instruction — The team method of instruction has been found to be the most efficient way in which to organize this curriculum. The entire senior class, which includes between 380 and 400 students, has been divided into 16 sections that meet every day during one of four periods. A team of four regular teachers, assisted by guest lecturers in music, art, history, and language, handles the classes. Large group instruction, in which 90 to 120 students meet together for a lecture or audio-visual presentation, is followed by individual work and discussion in small classes on the following day or days. Students are grouped by ability in the individual classes, and assignments and requirements based on the general lecture presentation are varied within the small group.

Course Requirements

Notebooks: Each student is required to keep a notebook containing lecture notes, reading notes, field trip reports, and his own papers. There is no textbook in this course, and the technique for orderly note-taking is basic to a cumulative understanding of the curriculum.

Short papers: Each student is required to respond in writing once a week to the material under discussion. These short papers may be an evaluation of an idea, auxiliary library research, analysis of the readings, or other material. The purpose of these short assignments is to force the student to articulate his thinking and to verbalize his ideas.

Term paper: Each student is required to write one resource paper of not less than 1,500 words, which conforms to exacting requirements of form and content. The paper must be fully annotated, show evidence of extensive investigation, and be supported by a wide variety of authoritative sources. The student may select any subject for investigation that derives from the content of the course. Such a scope is extremely wide indeed.

Creative activity: In addition to the term paper, each student is required to enter into a creative activity that will lead toward a tangible involvement with the arts. According to interests developed during the course, students may paint, sculpt, make films, write plays, go to museums, write or perform music, or engage in any similar activity that will increase their awareness of the creative process and their information about the arts. Our students are particularly fortunate to have the museums, theaters, and concert halls of New York City only an hour away by public transportation, and they take full advantage of this fact.

Course of Study — The River Dell humanities course has an anthropological and philosophical rather than an aesthetic and critical focus. Man's differences from other animals, his indefatigable efforts to understand cause and effect, the meaning of the universe, and his relationship with God and his fellow man are examined in terms of his religious and social ideas and art forms. Ideas, not chronology, form the core of each unit. The year is divided into four broad units, each of which represents a different approach to the same central problem of understanding mankind. The purpose of each unit is to examine the central human drives common to all men and to observe the extraordinary variations in culture that climate, terrain, language, and stage of development have brought about. Within each unit, the music and art of the culture being discussed are also examined so that students may understand something of their diverse functions and forms.

The four broad divisions for study during the year are:

1. Man's interpretation of forces outside himself, which considers a wide variety of religious ideas and their concomitant social implications (approximately three months).
2. The search for social order, which considers the opposing views of man's nature as seen in utopian versus manipulatory blueprints for the state (approximately two months).
3. The individual in society, which considers conformity and revolt, together with the emotional or intellectual reactions to environmental situations (approximately two months).
4. The current scene, which examines the phenomenon of alienation in today's Western society (approximately two months).

Within the major subjects divisions, the following ideas are examined:

I. Man's interpretation of forces outside himself
   A. Primitive religions: Early ideas of God as seen in primitive societies; the meaning of animism, ritual, magic, and daemonism
   B. Primitive art and primitive music: A discussion of primitive art and its function within the religious system; music as an expression of religious idea among

primitive peoples; the use of corporeal rhythms, chants, and incantations as part of ritual

C. Oriental religions: The Hindu view, with its social implications; Buddhism, Tao, Zen, and the renunciation of "earthly desires," Confucianism, the philosophy of harmonious relationships, and Yin and Yang; Shintoism, the concept of a "chosen people"

D. Oriental art, architecture and music: Their reflection and interpretation of oriental religion and culture

E. Ancient Greece: The foundation of the symbolic mythological system and the human characteristics of high gods

F. Man's relationship to the gods, as seen in Euripides' *The Bacchae* and Sophocles' *Oedipus the King*; the Greek view of destiny, free will, and fate

G. Greek theater as an expression of religious idea; the tragic hero

H. Greek art as an interpretation of cultural ideas concerning the nature of the universe and man's place in it; the feeling for harmony, balance, stasis, logic, and reason as the good as opposed to excess, violence, and extreme behavior; the classic/romantic antithesis

I. The Judeo-Christian value system
   1. Ancient Hebraic concepts of life and man's relationship to God; law, history, the fall, the Covenant
   2. The phenomenon of Zoroaster and the impact of Dualism on Judeo-Christian development
   3. The Christian religion, its foundations in Hebrew theology and the Christian view of man's role on earth and in the life hereafter; the Kerygma and the Logos

J. Christian culture in the West, after Rome
   1. The endurance of Christianity in the Western world through the institution and dogmas of the Church
   2. Music of the early church; the Mass and its musical setting
   3. Different epochs and attitudes in developing Chris-

tian thought as seen in painting, Byzantine through Renaissance; the rise of humanism

4. Architecture as an expression of idea from the early Romanesque to the late Gothic cathedral; Chartes
5. Religious symbolism and iconography in northern Renaissance painting
6. The medieval view of the order of life as expressed in Dante's *Divine Comedy;* the mixture of Greek and Christian ideas in the Sistine Chapel; Michelangelo film
7. The meaning of Luther's revolt against Church authority; the Reformation's altered view of the nature of man, God, and society as a precursor for the Enlightenment and modern times

II. The search for social order

A. The social drive of man toward a system that satisfies the human need for security, propagation of the species, comfort, relationship; the biological origin of man's social nature
B. Ethical concepts as a base for social order: The religious utopias and the growth of moral law; Eden, Brahman; the Codes of Moses, Hammurabi, Manu
C. Law as a man-made institution: Ideal concepts of the state as expressed in Plato's *Republic*
D. The state as an extension of man's basic drives: Ways in which the protective social order becomes an instrument of power; Machiavelli's *The Prince*
E. The real world: Types of social organizations, why they exist, how they operate; Orwell's *Animal Farm* in context with American utopian social experiments, the Marxists' social experiment
F. War: An instrument of the state or an expression of man's basic nature? Why do men fight? Robert Ardrey's *Territorial Imperative*

1. The artist looks at war — two views, one an expression of hero-worship and national pride, the other an expression of revulsion and horror

2. Music and its uses to stir patriotic sentiment or anti-war feeling; setting for Britten's *War Requiem*
3. The effects of war on both the individual and the state as expressed by Euripides in *The Trojan Women*
4. A great propaganda film from "the other side," *Alexander Nevsky*

III. The individual in society
   A. The temperament of the individual: The human instinct toward balance, form, and pattern as an aspect of the drive toward security, contrasted with the desire for change, search, and quest as an aspect of the drive toward knowledge or perfection
   B. The classic/romantic antithesis in art, architecture, literature and music; The Parthenon and the Gaudi Cathedral at Barcelona; Sonata-allegro form and the music of the 19th century; Pope's *Essay on Man*, and Whitman's *Leaves of Grass*.
   C. Individualism: A discussion of the meaning of individualism in modern times as contrasted with the individual in ancient societies; conservatism as an extreme form of classicism and anarchy as an extreme form of romanticism
   D. The mixture of opposing elements within the individual that affect his perception of good and evil; natural versus man-made law in Goethe's *Faust*
   E. Revolt: The individual's reaction to an environment that seems to permit values different from his own and that he can neither tolerate nor accept; Shakespeare's *Hamlet* (film also)
   F. Conformity: The revolt of the non-heroic individual in a society where conformity is a high value; Lewis's *Babbitt*
   G. Responsibility: The plight of the individual who sees beyond the narrow conventions of the group and endeavors to bring about change; Ibsen's *Enemy of the People*; what is the individual's responsibility to the group and to himself?

IV. The contemporary world and the rise of alienation and anxiety

    A. An examination of the effect of cultural disorientation on an individual giving rise to the question, "What is the basic nature of man?" Conrad's *Heart of Darkness*

    B. The clash of cultures: The individual in a foreign society as exemplified by Forster's *Passage to India*

    C. The accelerated pace of living: The loss of place and effectiveness as seen in Miller's *Death of a Salesman* (film also)

    D. *Wozzeck,* Alban Berg's musical expression of the incomprehensibility of man's role on earth

    E. The sense of despair: Futility in the post World War I era, as seen in Eliot's *The Wasteland* and *Hollow Men*

    F. Depersonalization in art in the modern era: pop, op, and the new view of nature

    G. The theater of today as a reflection of the times; Albee's *Zoo Story*

    H. Alienation as expressed in music; the new uses of pattern, accident, dissonance, and machines to produce meaningful sound

    I. A summing up: An analysis of our own culture in the stream of history and the current search for lasting values, with comment on the possible trends indicated by our art forms, our social ideas, and the state of our religious institutions.

Readings — All or part of the following titles are required reading for all students in the course. Titles distinguished by an asterisk are not read *in toto;* those marked by a # sign are either omitted or excerpted for terminal groups: * # Benedict, *Patterns of Culture*; Bradley, *Guide to the World's Religions,* * # Bouquet, *Comparative Religion*; # Rose, *Handbook of Greek Mythology*; * Hamilton, *Mythology*; Aeschylus, *Prometheus Bound*; Euripides, *The Bac-*

chae and *The Trojan Women*; Sophocles, *Oedipus the King*; Bible (O.T.) Genesis, Job; (N.T.) Matthew; * # Plato, *Republic*; * # Aristotle, *Poetics*; * # Dante, *Inferno*; # Machiavelli, *The Prince;* * # Aubrey, *Territorial Imperative*; # Goethe, *Faust,* Part I; Shakespeare, *Hamlet*; Voltaire, *Candide*; # Forster, *Passage to India*; Hesse, *Siddhartha*; Ibsen, *Enemy of the People*; Conrad, *Heart of Darkness*; Orwell, *Animal Farm*; Lewis, *Babbitt*; MacLeish, *J. B.*; Miller, *Death of a Salesman*; Albee, *Zoo Story*; * Cooper, *Learning to Listen*; and * Taylor, *Learning to Look.*

Materials and Resources — Because the scope of a humanities program is so wide, it is necessary to have available for students a quantity of books, prints, slides, and projection equipment. A separate collection of materials has been added to the library to augment the normal holdings in philosophy, religion, anthropology, archaeology, psychology, history, art, and music. In addition, sizeable collections of records, slides, prints, and filmstrips have been accumulated and are freely circulated to the students.

The proximity of our own community to New York City's vast resources is an added advantage to the program, although the collections of museums throughout the world are now available, second hand, to anyone in any locality through books and the various film media.

There is extensive use of multiple copies of paperback books for the required reading assignments. Since these books usually cost very little, a number of titles can be acquired for the price of one hard-cover text. Keeping track of these paperbacks is another story, however, and the friendship of a good librarian is an essential ingredient for control.

David E. Tabler

Interdisciplinary elective for college-bound seniors; concentrates on selected examples of intellectual and artistic expressions of Western man; lectures and small seminars but no independent work; daily double periods; special interest mini-courses offered during last three weeks.

Rationale — The humanities course at Ann Arbor Pioneer High School is a team-taught, interdisciplinary, double-credit elective for college-bound seniors who have an interest in participating in a different and intellectually challenging educational experience. Our course is quite frankly academic. We believe that no one course can do all things for all students, and our purpose is to develop some insight into the evolution of Western thought. We also offer a humanities course in American culture to students who do *not* plan to go to college, which is similar in design but entirely separate.

Objectives and Approach — Our approach is chronological; we begin with the Greeks and proceed to the modern era. Our method is that of "post-holing," that is, looking at selected, representative masterpieces in some depth rather than superficially surveying everything available. Thus, in determining our curriculum, the major problem is to determine what *not* to teach. There's a multitude of riches!

Our fundamental belief is that the condition of the society in which we live is determined by our collective past, and we thus have taken for our concern the past of Western man. We believe that man has, for some 2,500 years, pondered his condition on earth and has expressed his conclusions in various ways: painting, sculpture, architecture, music, literature, philosophical writings, and political and economic theory. We present our students with some outstanding and influential examples of these to demonstrate to them the importance of these human expressions in understanding our own ways of thought. We also examine with them the characteristics of the major forms of artistic self-expression. Our third purpose is to show that within a given era, political theorists, painters, sculptors, architects, dramatists, poets, and musicians may well use their particular media to express similar ideas. This interrelationship of content and form is very important to us. Hearing Mozart, seeing the gardens of Versailles, and reading Racine's *Phaedra* will give a deeper understanding of the concept of rationalism than will the examination of any of these in isolation. The similarities of musical structure and of poetic structure make each form clearer.

We believe very deeply in the individual integrity of each discipline. For this reason, we have a team of teachers. Art is taught by a qualified art teacher and music by a qualified music teacher. Likewise, the literature and history parts of the program are handled by teachers with majors in those areas. We also avoid the excessive use of one discipline to serve the purposes of another. The art teacher, for example, may show some slides of Greek pottery when Keats' "Ode on a Grecian Urn" is being studied under the direction of the English teacher, but she will also present Greek art as a subject worthy of study in its own right. The music teacher may play some Elizabethan lute music to set the mood for an examination of some aspect of *Hamlet,* but at another time, the secular music of the English Renaissance will be heard for its own sake.

Staff — The teaching team is made up of six teachers: one in art, one in music, two in history, and two in English. One teacher is designated as the team chairman, and he fulfills various functions: correlating the presentations in the various disciplines, printing a weekly schedule of assignments and activities, representing the team's interests in meetings of school department chairmen, keeping attendance and grade records, handling the budget allotted to the humanities program, and performing other activities of an administrative nature. He is not considered a master teacher and has no authority in terms of teacher evaluation or in the content presented by other teachers.

Schedule and Course of Study — The course consists of two semesters. The first semester ends with a consideration of the 17th century, and the second begins with the Age of Reason. Students may take either or both for credit, but the vast majority take both semesters. Thus a humanities student can earn one credit in English (Humanities serves as an alternative to the regular senior English course in English literature) and another in social studies. The latter grade is determined by averaging the student's work in art, history, and music. (The proportions are: art — 20%, history — 60%, and music — 20%.) For administrative purposes, each teacher arrives at a grade for each student and submits these grades to the team chairman, who averages them.

The class meets for two periods each day. The first period is a large group session where one of the teachers presents a lecture to the total class, which usually consists of 75 to 90 students. Of the five lecture periods each week, one is in art and one in music. The other three are divided between literature and history, alternating week to week, with one or two lectures. Lectures, by the way, are not always formal, academic presentations. They often turn into large group discussions or take the form of student or faculty panels. Lately we have used multi-media presentations involving art, music, and literary readings very successfully. We also have frequent special presentations by members of the high school faculty outside our program or by experts from the community or from the University of Michigan. All regular members of the teaching team are expected to attend all guest lectures.

The second period is devoted to seminars. The lecture group is divided into four small groups for the discussion of English and history readings. Each seminar group is assigned to a history teacher and an English teacher, who alternate meeting with the seminar four days a week. The fifth day (Wednesday) the second hour is used for a variety of activities: extra lectures in art and music, tests, impromptu theme writing, art or music discussions (since these teachers do not see the students in seminars), films, study or consultation time, or other activities.

Materials — The following readings are required: Homer, *The Odyssey*; Sophocles, *Oedipus the King*; Plato, *Phaedo*; *The Song of Roland* (an excerpt of about 1,000 lines); Chaucer, *The Canterbury Tales* ("General Prologue" and "The Pardoner's Tale"); Machiavelli, *The Prince*; Shakespeare, *Hamlet*; John Donne poetry; Book of Job; Milton, *Samson Agonistes*; Racine, *Phaedra*; Swift, *Gulliver's Travels*, book 4; Voltaire, *Candide*; Goethe, *Faust* part I; romantic poetry (about three weeks); either Flaubert, *Madame Bovary* or Dostoyevsky, *Crime and Punishment*; Ibsen, *A Doll's House*; modern poetry (about two weeks); Huxley, *Brave New World*; and one of the following; Conrad, *Heart of Darkness*; Camus, *The Stranger*; Golding, *Lord of the Flies*; or Paton, *Cry, the Beloved Country*.

Students also purchase Copland's *What to Listen for in Music* and Wold's and Cykler's *An Outline History of Music* for readings to supplement music lectures. The humanities department furnishes the following books a ratio of one to every two or three students: *Readings in Western Civilization*, edited by Knowles and Snyder, from which most of the history readings are taken; *Art Through the Ages* by Gardner, and *Learning to Look* by Taylor. Reading assignments to supplement the art lectures are given in these volumes.

For the last two years we have been experimenting with what we call mini-courses or special interest courses. During the last three weeks of the year, each team member offers a special short course. Each student enrolls in the course that most interests him. These classes are held in place of seminars, and large group presentations are continued during this period. Some of these courses have been concerned with jazz, painting and poetry, Negro literature, student revolutionaries, the theatre of the absurd, existentialism in drama, modern music, Marshall McLuhan, Utopian thought, and other topics. These have taken the place of the modern novel unit and the *Brave New World* unit, but these works are sometimes offered as special interest courses if there is sufficient student interest.

Conclusions — We try to open doors for students by introducing them to ideas and materials most of them have not encountered before. Because we see the course as mainly introductory, we do not encourage individual research projects, and by limiting ourselves to academic roles, we do not include any studio work in art or music. If we have talented students (and we usually have many), we draw upon their talents in playing or singing to enrich class presentations, but we do not teach these things within the confines of our course. Ample opportunity is available elsewhere in the school curriculum for studio experiences.

Most of the teachers who work with the humanities program describe it as the most exciting teaching they have ever done. In eight years, our enrollment has risen from about 80 to nearly 170 students. We now have two separate sections. Many of the students presently enrolled are younger brothers and sisters of previous students. These facts alone indicate that most find it a richly rewarding experience.

Morris Saxe

Geared to students' concerns and questions; emphasizes human values and ideas; flexible, changing, open-ended content; grades and tests minimized; multi-media experiences and field trips; full-year elective for seniors; double periods; team-teaching.

Rationale — Need for a humanities course existed for both students and teachers. Correlation of and interaction between different disciplines were rare, and too much student effort was being expended to achieve grades to please teachers or parents. The emphasis since Sputnik in 1957 on acceleration and concentration on content, especially in math and science, had produced a climate in which learning was often a grim, joyless, and rather competitive business. An antidote was needed — an emphasis on human ideas and values and the recognition that the development of attitudes, skills, and understandings can be more important than the contents of a given course or just acquisition of knowledge. A way of thinking, living, and being was missing to a large degree.

History — In 1963 the desirability, indeed the necessity, for a course in humanities at Northport was realized. Active support and understanding by the school principal has been literally a *sine qua non* for the program. Each year of the program unpredictable situations have come up that called for extreme flexibility and forgiveness: frequent field trips, controversial books and topics, unexpected outside speakers, experiments in grading and other procedures, "lost" classes, sudden demands for more and different paperbacks, and juggling teacher schedules to allow interested science, math, and art teachers to make their contributions.

The superintendent also gave encouragement, plus support of a visible nature: two teachers were placed on salary during a summer to read, study, and develop a course of study.

Leaning heavily on humanities course outlines from other schools, the two teachers, one English and one social science, projected initially a cultural history of mankind, chiefly Western man. The story of man would be treated in six or seven periods (the Biblical world, the Greek world, etc.), and the humanities class would learn how the great ideas of each of these periods found expression in literature, art, music, and so on. Fortunately for their students and for them, the two planners became frightened by the enormity and conceit of this super-intellectual farrago, and they decided to scuttle this plan.

Fearing that any chronological approach would be too restrictive and having weighed and found wanting the merits of thematic organization, basic-textbook-as-guide methodology, and a current-issues orientation approach, they simply determined to plunge right in with an exciting play that would capture the interest of the students, *Death of a Salesman*. Then playing it by ear, i.e., learning the capabilities, interests, and aptitudes of the students and observing their reactions closely, they felt free to move backwards and forward in time, selecting for study those areas that seemed most apposite. They soon stopped being embarrassed over the fact that there seemed to be no rationale for the order in which some experiences were pursued; they learned that there are more important things to think about: How do you induce active student participation from those who sit in quotidian passivity, poised with notebook and pen, ready to write down the "answers"? How do you convince students who've been dealing with teachers' questions through 11 years of school that such questions are really ancillary and that it's *their* questions we really want? How can teachers discipline themselves to keep quiet and have the patience to wait for those questions? How does one create the human climate of mutual forgiveness that will encourage the emergence of the real questions? There were many more hows.

Objectives — Northport High School wanted a course:

1. Where there would be no hurry and no pressure to cover prescribed materials or to prepare for ritualistic examinations, one that could deal with *students'* concerns and questions, a course that could stay with any topic as long as class members were interested.
2. That could bring together some parts of a fragmented curriculum so that students and teachers could see that music, biology, literature, physics, and art all speak about the miracle and tragedy of being a human being.
3. Where "The proper study of man is man," where *human* values, be they in architecture, religion, or psychology, are a fit subject for study.
4. Where grades and tests would be practically eliminated as factors of importance, where students would work not to receive high scores but because they wanted to confront something in themselves and in the materials being investigated.
5. Where students would be the doers, a course open-ended enough so that they could determine some part of the curriculum.
6. With an environment not for the elite but for students of all interests and abilities.

All these objectives have not yet been achieved, but to a large extent, we have been successful with most of them and have begun to see our way toward those aims that have eluded us.

Approach — Although we have used teacher lectures to introduce units of study, to give background, or to lead groups through some esoteric areas, e.g., problems in translation in the Old Testament or the nature of id, ego, superego, more and more we have been relying on students, individually and in groups, to present material to the class. Group discussion has, from the beginning, remained the basic technique, and that's why double periods became essential. Viewing slides and films, listening to tapes and records, going on field trips, hearing visiting speakers, putting on and watching performances — such protean experiences have been a constant feature of our humanities program.

Some themes and ideas have been used every year, some only once, and not every section in a given year has been offered the same experiences. Although we try to avoid a superficial, dilettante approach (Warning to humanities teachers: Beware of becoming a cicerone!), we do not pretend to be exhaustive in our study. We are not offering a college course. We do not hesitate to use the cliché of "opening doors" to describe our course. Perhaps some of our students will open wide some of these doors and pursue in depth a newly developed interest.

Course of Study — Following are *some* of the themes, units or whatchamacallems — with *some* of the works we read and *some* of the guide questions. In many units bibliographies for additional suggested reading were made available.

I. Why the humanities? What are they?
   A. Reading[1]: essays in *Mirrors of Man*, edited by Paul
      C. Obler, New York: American Book Co., 1962: Louis
      B. Salomon, "How Important Are the Humanities?"

---

1. NOTE: The class was given frequent, short, objective quizzes dealing with details and seemingly trivial matter in their reading. The purpose of these quizzes was to help students learn to read closely. We stressed the importance of knowing exactly what an author says, before the implication of what he is saying can be discussed intelligently. We wanted to minimize top-of-the-head thinking.

George Boas, "The Problem of the Humanities," and Stringfellow Barr, "Liberal Education, a Common Adventure."

B. Guide questions were used to direct the reading through difficult materials, to stimulate discussion, and to bring out ideas traditionally presented in lecture form. As time went on and as students brought forth their own questions, there was less reliance on the guide questions.

1. What are some of the great concerns of modern man?
2. What are some of the great ideas and movements of this century that may have brought about these concerns?
3. What is the relationship of science to the humanities?
4. How can we use both to come to grips with life?
5. Are the classics still important in education?
6. What are some reasonable educational ideals for free men?

II. A modern playwright views the human condition.

A. Reading: Arthur Miller, *Death of a Salesman*

B. Guide questions:

1. What are some of the problems of modern man as presented in this play?
2. What are the values of modern society as Miller sees them?
3. Are the Lomans really a "sick" family?
4. Which characters are psychologically "whole"?
5. What does Uncle Ben represent?
6. What is the real tragedy in this play?
7. What is the playwright's judgment of the acceptance of middle-class values?

C. Assignment: A paper in which students react to, or evaluate the play, was required. Suggested topics were given, but students were free to write about whatever went on in their minds as we read and discussed the play. For these assignments that wound up each unit, students were encouraged to express themselves in media other than writing. They learned that it was appropriate and desirable to express their thoughts and emotions with paint, in sculpture, in music, on film, on tape, and in oral presentations.

III. A classic playwright views the human condition.

A. Readings: *The Oedipus Plays of Sophocles*, translated by Paul Roche, and *Mythology* by Edith Hamilton

B. Guide questions:

1. Are these simply interesting stories, or do they tell us something about the human lot?

2. In the Greek view, does man have free will?

3. Was Oedipus guilty of hubris? How? Was Creon? Antigone?

4. Who was more of a victim, Oedipus or Willy Loman?

5. What kind of woman was Jocasta? Why did she commit suicide? Why did Oedipus not commit suicide?

6. Was Oedipus' punishment commensurate with his crime?

7. Was Antigone involved in civil disobedience in defying Creon's edicts? Compare with modern examples of the same activity.

8. What do these plays say about the finite and infinite qualities of human existence?

IV. The Old Testament[2]. What ideas and values does it present about humanity?

A. Reading: The Old Testament. Any verison was acceptable. We studied closely all of Genesis, the first 20 chapters of Exodus, also Amos, Jonah, and Micah. Findings of recent archaeological and Semitic studies in the Middle East were presented as background ma-

---

2. NOTE: This was not a religious or a tendentious study; emphasis was on the literary and historical. Our purpose in taking up this unit was not that pupils should know the sources of quotations they encounter in their general reading, but that they might learn to read an important book of our Western civilization.

terial, a comparison was made with other Near Eastern creation accounts, and the pros and cons of the Critical Documentary Theory were investigated.

B. Guide questions:

1. What are the problems involved in reading and translating an ancient, dilapidated text?

2. What are the chief themes of the narrators of Genesis?

3. How does the Old Testament view of the historical process differ from that of the Greeks?

4. Compare the Old Testament account of creation with those of ancient Egypt and Babylonia. What are the significant differences?

5. How do the Biblical narrators account for the beginning of wrong-doing and evil?

6. What is the Old Testament concept of election?

7. What evidence can we find that the Patriarchs were or were not monotheistic?

8. How does history, as given in the Old Testament differ from modern, secular history? To what extent is the purpose of each different?

9. What new concepts of the relationship of man to man and man to God are found in the literary prophets? What new view of YHWH do they present?

10. What insights into human nature can be attained from a study of the Scriptures?

V. Psychology and the human condition.

A. Reading[3]: Freud, *Civilization and Its Discontents*, translated by James Strachey.

B. Guide questions:

1. How does the "father of modern psychology" view

---

3. NOTE: There has been less dealing with the themes of the text more recently as classes have found it more worthwhile to study the effects of Freud and psychology on other areas. Panels of students did research and presentations about dreams, psychological tests, hypnosis, Freudian influence on art, music, and film, psychology and religion, and sex education. As in earlier years, the class had the opportunity to listen to visiting Freudian and non-Freudian psychologists interpret Freud's work.

human beings in relation to the constrictions imposed by modern society?

2. Why is man's instinctual nature in opposition to the demands of society?

VI. Education at Northport High School [4].

A. Informal debates were based on the following questions:

1. What are Northport High School students really like?
2. Are we producing mediocre students at Northport?
3. How good is the curriculum at Northport High School?
4. How effective is the program for non-academic students?
5. How good is the faculty at Northport High School?

Space restrictions preclude accounts of other topics, but here are some that proved fruitful: Human values in architecture and city planning, alienation (Faulkner's *Light in August*; Camus' *The Stranger*; Conrad's *Heart of Darkness*), science and the humanities, primitive man, existentialism, and ballet dancing.

Music has been a year-long unit in our program, giving greater meaning to various ideas and topics we experienced.

Class field trips are conducted each year to the New York City museums, especially the Museum of Modern Art, the Whitney, the Guggenheim, and the Metropolitan. A Greek play, *Medea*, or a modern one, Pinter's *The Homecoming*, gives dramatic impact to what we discuss in class. A walking architectural tour on Fifth and Sixth Avenues lends life to classroom treatment of architecture and city planning.

On these group trips, the school bus becomes a classroom on wheels. Students or teachers use portable PA systems to make presentations pertinent to the activity and to point out highlights en route. Different roads, bridges, and ferries

---

4. NOTE: This topic came from student interest. Students worked in small groups, did research through questionnaires, interviews, and class visitation, and presented informal debates.

are used on each trip to the city to give students a feeling for all parts of the metropolis.

Individual field trips are also part of the course. Why should an entire class go to something that interests one or two students only or that does not lend itself to mass invasion? Why does a teacher always have to tag along? The classroom is everywhere, and individualization in learning means just that.

Staff and Scheduling — Various ways have been explored to deal with logistical aspects of the program. Each year it has been a full-year elective for seniors, and up to 1967–68 each student earned one full credit for English and one for social studies. A double period block of time was devoted to the class five days per week, although the class did not always meet for both periods, nor did it necessarily meet every day once we were fully under way.

Two teachers worked with 39 students the first year. The following September 90 students were working with four teachers — two teachers per section of 45 students, with each section overlapping one of the two double periods, coming together in one large group when desirable and often going their separate ways. Four teachers with some 100 students, all in the same double period of time, marked the third year's endeavor and allowed for great flexibility in grouping. However, problems and personality conflicts within the team (Teachers are really human.) prevented this arrangement from realizing its full potential. During the year 1967–68 two teachers worked with 70 students and tried a single period arrangement with one credit for English or social studies. The one period limitation proved unsatisfactory; two periods are more functional.

To date those directly involved in the teams have been English and social studies teachers (one with a rich background in art) and one music teacher. Members of other departments have contributed for as much as a week at a time on standby and guest lecturer basis.

Evaluation — We have had many misgivings and doubts about our procedures and choice of materials; we could descant in dismal detail about our problems and flounderings and flops, but we have shed our hesitation about the basic nature of our course. In spite of the looseness of the program and the groping of the teachers, our students (and their parents) have been generally responsive and enthusiastic. Such a course we now know is needed.

Some of our students say they are still ". . . not sure what humanities is . . ." and many of their questions are still unanswered, but it requires no computer to measure the meaning the humanities experiences has had for many of them. One student summarized it succinctly: "The course for me was frustrating, exciting, meaningful, and most enjoyable. I entered the course knowing most everything and left it knowing that I knew nothing. Learning is now an exciting thing. Humanities was learning."

Conclusions —To have a humanities course for a small, elite group seems fraudulent and antithetical to the spirit of humanities. Hence Northport is seeking ways to broaden the humanities idea in education. For the same reason we are humanizing the contents of our courses in English, social studies, science, music, and art. Where possible, we are attempting a number of ways to humanize the interpersonal relationships within the school. Ultimately, not a humanities course but a humanities school is what is needed.

Whether the humanities course is a catalyst or simply a symptom of this humanizing syndrome may be an academic question. We do know that the program is expanding next year. A team of two teachers is planning a humanities program for the terminal student. Another team consisting of English, art, and music teachers is now engaged in planning a regular humanities course that will be markedly different from what has been taking place heretofore. (This is one reason why it's advisable, especially in humanities, to have new people move into a program and to let those who've done their bit move on to other pastures.) No longer will we be taking mincing steps in the direction of art and music. They will be a part of the course as much as literature.

It's not humanities simply because one integrates music, art, and literature within a course. That may have merit, perhaps, but humanities happen when students and teachers seeking leads to the tantalizing enigmas of "Who am I?" or "Why art?" or "What's happening to me?" look for meanings in literature and drama, in music and dance, or in painting and sculpture to answer these questions.

Morris S. Buske

Two-year "World Civilization" course for ninth- and tenth-graders of average ability; history, art, and music teachers; large and small group instruction; comparisons, critical analysis, research, and tolerance of differences stressed; heavy use of films and tapes.

History and Rationale — "World Civilization" differs from most humanities courses in that (1) it is history oriented, and (2) it is offered to ninth- and tenth-graders of average ability. The course grew out of local need for a history course for freshmen of average ability. "World History" was rejected, since as traditionally taught the course would have been difficult for first-year high school students. A new course was devised: a two-year sequence, based on world history and chronologically organized, but combining work in music, art, and philosophy with history. The first year corresponds roughly with the first semester of "World History," and the second year with the second semester of "World History."

Objectives — Objectives of the "World Civilization" course have been modified somewhat since its inception in 1967. Originally the course was history centered; today it is more nearly a humanities course that is history oriented. Students are led to look for answers to three key questions: "What is man?" "What is society?" and "What is the universe?" An attempt is made to foster attitudes of tolerance for differences, cosmopolitanism, respect for the sanctity of life, respect for the rights of the individual, respect for property and group rights, and self-awareness. Research skills and a habit of critical analysis are among the skills developed. An effort is made to encourage student creativity and independence of thought by making the teacher's role one of definer, formulator, and discussion leader, a co-seeker of the truth. History still forms an important part of the course work but now with the goal of helping students see how society has evolved and how the individual has fared in different environments. An examination of the course's organization and materials may bring its objectives into sharper focus.

Students and Staff — Students in "World Civilization" are drawn from the top eighty percent of the freshman class; only applicants with serious reading or related difficulties are excluded. During the sophomore year, students may continue with the second year of "World Civilization" or may elect the second semester of "World History." Those who take all four semesters of "World Civilization" receive history credit or, if present plans materialize, may gain credit for three semesters of history and one semester of fine arts should they so desire.

Flexible scheduling permits both large group instruction and work in smaller groups of various sizes. On most Mondays and Wednesdays the students meet in large sections for films and lectures. The remaining days of the week are devoted to discussions and other activities in classes of normal size, in smaller groups, or in combinations of two classes.

A team, including an art teacher, a music teacher, and eight members of the history department, is responsible for the teaching. Their fields of specialization make possible the study of each culture or period from several angles. For example, the unit on Greece combines work in Greek history, art, music, philosophy, and literature. Lectures, viewing films and filmstrips, reading excerpts from Greek plays, philosophy, and history, producing a play, and analyzing Greek architecture all aim at developing an in-depth understanding of classical Greece.

Course of Study

Unit 1: The freshman year opens with a six-weeks examination of our society, with an emphasis on value systems developed through various activities and media. Slides taken locally illustrate differing architectural styles that were influenced by construction dates and individual tastes. Films (*Nothing But a Man, The Hustler, 16 in Webster Groves*) point up the problems and values of diverse parts of our society, and a showing of TV commercials illustrates the concepts advertisers have about the nature of our society. Readings include excerpts from Studs Terkel's *Division Street* and other materials designed to heighten awareness of the modern scene. At the close of the unit, the student is asked to draw up a plan for a model city.

Unit 2: This aims to establish the prehistoric parallel. *Lord of the Flies* is read in connection with a study of prehistoric society and the emergence of civilizations in the ancient Middle East.

Unit 3: Several films in the Encyclopaedia Britannica humanities series are seen in this unit on Greece. Students read and discuss *Oedipus Rex, Antigone*, Plato's *Apology*, and the section on Athens in Fenton's *Three Cities*. An art project is based on illustrating a Greek quotation by means of a montage, although, as an alternative, some students present *The Trojan Women* in simplified form or do other projects. The unit ends with a survey of Roman history.

Unit 4: The second semester begins with work on the Middle Ages. Bodo the Peasant and Madame Eglentyne (from Power's *Medieval People*) are discussed as representative of people living at that time, and medieval art and architecture

143

are studied to show how man then viewed society and the universe.

Unit 5: The transition from medieval to modern times is handled by reading *Utopia* and Brecht's *Galileo*. In connection with *Utopia,* each student is asked to draw up a plan for an ideal society.

Unit 6: This unit on the Renaissance centers around the material on Florence in Fenton's *Three Cities.* Britannica films and art and music lectures stress the growing importance of the individual.

Unit 7: This unit involves study of the religions of the West. Ross and Hills's *Great Religions by Which Men Live* is read, and local clergymen come to the school to speak about their faiths. Students are encouraged, as a project, to devise their own religions.

Unit 8: The final unit of the freshman year returns to the present with the film, *On the Waterfront,* and the study of New York from *Three Cities.*

Work in the sophomore year, in process of revision, includes the following: Unit 1: The world of 1780; Unit 2: Revolutions; Unit 3: Nationalism, Imperialism, Racism; Unit 4: Industrialism; Unit 5: New Images of Man; and Unit 6: War and Catastrophe.

Readings include Hayes and Faissler's *Modern Times* and Hanscom, Henerman and Posmer's *Voices of the Past,* volume 3. As in the first year, films are used extensively, and the method of comparison helps to highlight differences in attitudes and achievements. For example, Bishop's *Day in the Life of JFK* is compared with Saint-Simon's *Day in the Life of the King,* and selections from Galbraith's *Affluent Society* are read in conjunction with the section on mercantilism in Colbert's *Memoirs.*

Art and music lectures in both years relate to the unit of work being done and also seek to develop a coherent program of understanding and appreciation in these two fields. In music, for example, an attempt is made to reach students not only through lectures but also through listening to a series of tapes that have been prepared for the course through the cooperation of the Data Retrieval System at the high school. Students listen to the tapes in carrels in the retrieval center during free periods. Additional elements of the course include some field trips, e.g., to Frank Lloyd Wright's designed homes in Oak Park, and occasional faculty lecturers who speak about their special fields of expertise.

Conrad Stawski
Elective for seniors of average and better ability; team-taught by English instructors; survey and analysis of art forms and exposure to art experiences; individual creative projects; guest lecturers, multi-media, and field trips.

Approach and Objectives — The humanities course at Hickman High School is an elective available to seniors of average or better ability and achievement who wish to broaden their familiarity with and understanding of the arts. Basically the course is a survey and analysis of such factors in art as subject and source, elements, mediums, function, style, form, and organization. The intent is to develop the aesthetic and critical ability of the student, to expose him to a wide range of art experiences, and to enrich his responses by showing relationships underlying the various arts and offering him the opportunity to achieve his own synthesis. This basic approach, however, is modified with attempts at historical perspectives, "types" studies, and a study of cultural and philosophical values. The basic approach follows the pattern of the state curriculum guide, *The Allied Arts: A High School Humanities Guide for Missouri,* and the McGraw-Hill textbook, *The Humanities* by Dudley and Faricy. Further modifications are shaped by additional readings, some of which are listed below.

Course of Study — In addition to the text and supplementary readings, the course makes use of slides, filmstrips, records, movies, and opaque projections. Typical art lectures, usually accompanied by slides, may cover such areas as: Egyptian and Greek architecture as reflection of cultural ideals; various historical styles in architecture, from antiquity through the Middle Ages to the present; various mediums in painting and sculpture; form and structure in the visual and other arts; the study of individual artists in reference to historical and personal style, e.g., Michelangelo, Wyeth, and Picasso; the relative value of terms such as realism, distortion, and abstraction.

In addition to formal lectures of the type suggested above, the course is always discussing broader problems in the philosophy of aesthetics, such as: "What is art?" "How does surrealism relate to the Apollonian-Dionysian contrast in art?" "What are or seem to be valid standards of judgment?" "How does the new in architecture relate to the expression of cultural values and material realities of the age?" And, of course, whenever possible the students are led to find relationships among the various arts. For example, to see how medium conditions art, students examine three nocturnes — Van Gogh's *Starry Night, Clare de Lune* by Debussy, and the poem, "Silver," by Walter de la Mare — and then draw conclusions on the strengths and limitations of the various mediums used. Or students will look at Romeo and Juliet in the form of Shakespeare's play and compare it to the Zefferelli film and its musical treatments by Berlioz and Tschaikowsky. Students might be asked to trace the function of the rational faculty as a cultural ideal of the Greeks in their philosophy, their architecture, and their drama. Or they might be asked to observe how a Renaissance artist such as Michelangelo drew upon classic civilizations in his sculpture and architecture and where he transcended those influences.

Requirements — Each student must submit a project during the second semester. Resource papers are accepted as substitutes from students who claim absolutely no creative talent, but every effort is made to encourage students to produce a creative or original piece in one of the arts. These have varied tremendously in type and quality over the years. Among some of the projects submitted in the past have been musical compositions, including sonatas and numbers of theme and variation pieces, mosaics, modern dance interpretations, mobiles, studies in various mediums, collections of poetry, and books of children's stories. Some outstanding individual pieces recently were a new, eclectic religion called "Infinitism," a wire sculpture of a nude, a theme and variations for piano in baroque, classic, romantic, and contemporary styles, a remarkably faithful and careful copy of a Byzantine madonna in mosaic, and a two-hour taped study of the history of jazz.

Resources — Where possible, the course draws upon local sources. Students hear occasional guest lecturers, take local and regional field trips, and attend local productions. For example, students have listened to University of Missouri professors speak on such subjects as religion, Platonic and Aristotelian philosophy, and Greek archeology; they have visited the University Archeological Museum, the Saarinen Chapel at Stephens College, and the art museums in St. Louis and Kansas City; they have heard artist Sidney Larson explain his mural commissioned by a local firm; they have attended Stephens College productions of *Madame Butterfly* and *Romeo and Juliet*; and they have explained their religious beliefs and practices to foreign students.

The course tries to apply classroom experience to local reality; for example, students see slides of their own school building and of other local buildings to see how these incorporate classical or other architectural styles.

Methodology and Instruction — Since its inception six years ago, the course has been taught by a team of two teachers, both English instructors. A part of the English department, the course currently enrolls six large sections from among a student body of over 1,800. The teachers have experimented considerably with the course, within the traditional scheduling of five 55-minute per week sessions. They have tried both Kettering/I/D/E/A/ packages and short form packages and have provided opportunities for large group, seminar, and independent study as instructional techniques. Students are asked to buy four paperbacks to supplement the textbook. Currently these are *Religions of Man* by Huston Smith, *The Oedipus Plays of Sophocles* edited by Paul Roche, *Dialogues of Plato* edited by Justin Kaplan, and *Passage to India* by E. M. Forster. Titles have varied in the past, but the Sophocles and Plato have become standards for the work on Greek civilization. Enrichment suggestions in various units offer additional reading opportunities, as do seminar and panel experiences. Since the course is offered by the English department in addition to, rather than in lieu of, three other options for seniors, efforts are made to coordinate it with other courses. Although writing and other communication experiences are encouraged, the humanities program does not provide formal instruction in composition.

Since the teaching team handling the course has remained the same and no attempt has been made to rigidly standardize the course, a syllabus has not been produced. However, requests for sample materials have been honored, and while they are not reproduced in quantity specifically for distribution, a random collection of materials used in the past has been made available. Study guides, tests, packages, lecture outlines, and similar items in limited supply may be requested from Conrad Stawski, Chairman, English Department, Hickman High School, 1104 N. Providence Road, Columbia, Missouri 65201.

Sister Mary Sharon, SSND
Stresses experiences with and integration of the arts of Western and non-Western world, grades based on class participation — no tests; multi-media, field trips, and demonstrations; flexible content geared to seniors' backgrounds; monthly individual creative projects.

Rationale and Approach — The humanities program at St. Maria Goretti High School attempts to provide all graduates with a sampling of the arts and an integration of humanistic disciplines not usually achieved in other courses. It endeavors to give the student a world view of the arts, to unify the basic values taught in various subject areas, and to provide a basis for further explorations by the student in his future life.

The method used is experiential; students are exposed to as many experiences as possible. Projects that involve students in creative activities are assigned. Films, records, tapes, field trips, and demonstrations are the basic teaching approaches. Student discovery rather than teacher exposition is stressed. Flexibility is also an important element, since the course is tailored yearly to its place in the curriculum as well as its relevance to the particular group who will be taking it. Each summer the instructor studies the incoming group, evaluates their previous course experiences, their general background, and so on, and then revamps the course accordingly.

Students and Instructor — At present the course is offered to seniors only. It carries full credit and is taught daily for 50-minute periods, five days a week throughout the year. In the past, it was presented in three different ways to determine its best curricular placement: (1) as an elective open to both general and college prep seniors grouped heterogeneously — about 35 in all (1966–67); (2) as an elective open to both general and college prep seniors in separate sections (1967–68); and (3) as the required senior social studies credit (1968–69). The mixed groupings of numbers 1 and 3 were more productive and easier to teach. The slower, non-art oriented students were stimulated by the brighter, more aesthetically inclined. The author prefers number 3 because students were more self-motivated by the fact that all had to have the credit. They worked harder, produced better work, and seemed to enjoy the course more since it was ". . . not only fun but counted." (The quote is from an evaluation paper.)

The course is unusual in that it is taught by an individual with a B.A. in English, a minor in art, plus graduate work in theater, speech, and film. Guest lecturers, demonstrators in music and dance, field trips, and many films have made the broad spectrum possible.

Requirements — Students are required to complete assigned creative projects at approximately monthly intervals. Short reading or listening assignments are given almost daily. No tests are administered. Grades are based on class participation and projects. Students are given several choices of project content as well as types, on each assignment. Thus broad allowance is made for individual differences in both ability and interest.

Materials and Activities — There is no student text, but a large general selection of paperbacks correlated to the various units taught are available in sets of ten or 20. *Life* reprints in sets of 20 are also used. Films, slides, and records form the bulk of the teaching materials. A fee of $5 (This is a private school.) is charged each enrolling student to cover the cost of film rental, the purchase of needed project supplies, and to augment the supply of paperbacks and reprints. The humanities collection is growing since all materials are loaned to the students.

Student projects, both individual and class, have included demonstrations, oral reports, slide shows, 8mm filmmaking, audio-tapes, dramatizations, creative artwork such as sculpture and woodcarving, field trips, museum visits, research papers, creative poetry, and still photography.

Course of Study — As a result of the summer tailoring process and previous student evaluations of the course, the three years of the humanities program has produced in three different course outlines. Basically the areas of content have remained the same. Organization of material and individual selections have changed according to the group and the placement. The basic content areas are:

1. Survey of various forms of art: music, dance, visual arts, theater, screen arts.
2. Exploration of the non-Western world via the arts.
3. Exploration of our Western heritage, Greece to the Renaissance via the arts.
4. Confrontation with the world of 20th century man via the arts today.

The three general organizational plans were:

1966–67: Each separate art form was traced chronologically from its incipiency through its development in various cultures, both Oriental and Western, to the present day.

1967–68: Following a short introductory unit on the arts in general, the two semesters were devoted to distinct studies of non-Western culture, focusing on India, China, Japan, and Africa, and Western heritage, focusing on art development from ancient Greece to the American 20th century.

1968–69: Again a general introduction to the humanities presented the "Six Basic Directions of Creativity" by focusing on subject, source, medium, elements, and form in the six basic arts. Unit 2 surveyed the non-Western world including China, Japan, India, and Africa. The method varied from previous ones in that the four basic religions, all of which originated in the East, were used as pivots rather than the arts. Hinduism, Buddhism, Islam, and Christianity were studied and contrasted, and their influence on the arts was explored. The second semester devoted to Western heritage adopted a thematic approach. Its three units incorporated all the arts to reveal man's basic beliefs and hopes. Unit 3, "The City — Problems and Praises" focused on the "good life" of the "good man" in Athens, Florence, and New York. Unit 4, "The Comic Spirit" analyzed various types of humor in all the art forms and the psychological implications of man as humorist. Unit 5, "Man in Conflict" explored war as a phenomenon of man's existence.

Conclusion — Having taught many other high school subjects, the author can say without hesitation that the humanities course is not only the most rewarding course to teach but the one students enjoy the most. Each term students are asked to evaluate the course anonymously and objectively. Overwhelmingly the results are always positive. One question they answer asks, "Would you recommend this course to others?" In three years, after 150 students, no one has yet answered "No."

When asked to say what they have liked the most, invariably the answers include: the non-testing form of grading; the stress on experience rather than lecture-listening; and the integration of all the disciplines into a unified whole.

I feel strongly that in our small, semi-rural area high school, the place of a humanities course is undisputed. It fulfills a need our students have and provides an enjoyable experience with the arts that many of these students will continue on their own.

William F. Hamilton
Professional and student monthly auditorium presentations of drama, music, dance, art, literature, poetry, or a combination of these arts for all juniors and seniors; pre- and post-classroom discussions; cooperation with near-by college in cultural activities.

Rationale and Objectives — The Lakewood High School humanities program, supported entirely by local funding, is in its fifth year. The basic format has been incorporating large group instruction with normal classroom assignments. Our goal of making man more human is an elusive one. However, in this world where all people are struggling with a search for their own meaning, the effort continues to be challenging and rewarding.

The success and challenge of the Lakewood High School humanities program is making it meaningful for all students. This belief is buttressed by a report of a New Jersey Committee on Education written more than one hundred years ago: "Mind is immortal. Mind is imperial. It bears no mark of high or low, or rich or poor. It asks but freedom. It requires but light." We also agree with Dr. Bernard Knox that: "Never before have the humanizing elements of the humanities been more necessary to hold together the anonymous world in which we live." And with Dr. Robert Streeter's view that: "If we persist in our humanity, we shall remain humanists."

Approach, Instructors, Requirements, and Activities — The mechanics are simple: a major large group class experience is offered in the auditorium approximately once a month in the areas of drama, music, dance, art, literature, poetry, or a combination of these arts. Prior to the presentation, a printed description of the content of the program is distributed to humanities teachers. Appended to it are suggested approaches to aid teachers in their preparation and follow-up classes. Teachers of English and social studies usually alternate presentation months. However, depending on the event, teachers of other disciplines — art, music, drama and dance — may also participate in pre- or post-instruction classes.

The amount of preparation largely depends upon the type of experience. For example, prior to the week's visit of a composer-in-residence, English and music teachers presented information to help students understand electronic music; but prior to a presentation of "Arete," a combined arts experience, no prior preparation was given — the faculty wanted the students to experience and articulate their own reactions. Thus, class time was reserved after the performance for student discussion and argument. The teachers also incorporate large group presentations into their normal curriculum. For example, American literature teachers dealt with the poetry of Langston Hughes prior to a presentation of a stage offering entitled *The Langston Hughes Album,* by Karamu House Theater, an integrated community center. The players in the production spent the entire day in the classrooms discussing the poetry of Hughes with the students.

We have purposely offered humanities experiences to *all* 1,800 juniors and seniors at Lakewood High School. We believe this basic concept valid, for it is by studying mankind's achievements as a whole that one can understand himself.

Scheduling

At present a committee of six teachers of music, art, drama, literature, dance, and social studies plan and coordinate the program. (It is anticipated that this committee will be enlarged by an equal number of students this year.) The programs selected for presentation are recommended by individual members of the committee, and the committee uses one criterion for acceptance — Will this program contribute to the understanding of man and his endeavors in the world? The next step is to find out whether departments will be willing to prepare the programs.

Content, Resources, and Materials

Programs consist of professional presentations, and, because students should not only be viewers but participants, there are student presentations of various types.

For the past two years Lakewood High School has cooperated with Baldwin-Wallace College Humanities Institute in Berea, Ohio. Lakewood High School teachers and administrators have participated in planning various programs offered by the Institute on the college campus. Students have attended and participated in dramatic, musical, and discussion programs in which Baldwin-Wallace faculty and student groups as well as visiting guest artists have taken part.

Following is a listing of the programs for the years 1967–68 and 1968–69: Karamu Theater: *Spoon River Anthology*, dramatic reading and folk music; Lakewood High School Choirs and Orchestra: Thanksgiving day music; Cleveland Ballet Guild: "Training of a Classical Ballet Dancer," lecture-demonstration; composer Donald Erb at Lakewood one entire week: a study in contemporary music and poetry; Baldwin-Wallace Theatre: excerpts from *A Man for All Seasons*; Baldwin-Wallace Festival of the Arts; buffo opera: *La Serva Patrona*; film: *In Search of Man*; Lakewood High School modern dance group; Karamu Theater: "A Langston Hughes Album," a stage presentation and class discussion for entire day; films: student-made films and Daniel Hodermarsky, lecturer; and Dr. Frank Hurley: "The Harmony of Things Unlike: Music and Art."

Neil Van Steenbergen
Full-year honors course for gifted and academically talented seniors; modified team-teaching; three 12-week units in political philosophy, the arts, and man, society, and values; seminar-discussion techniques; spring weekend retreat extends classroom exchanges and readings; one-semester non-honors course also offered.

Background — In a society where relevance in curriculum is almost a universal student demand, it is significant that the humanities program at Millikan High School developed primarily from student interest. The course began with one class as a one semester senior seminar in social studies in the spring of 1961. The stimulus for that initial class came from a group of a dozen students who met regularly in the evenings to read poetry and plays, to discuss issues, and to probe and play with ideas. 1960 was the time of Sputnik and acceleration in science and math, and equal acceleration and depth in the social sciences was also needed. Technology is important and material success is a part of our way of life, but questions of value, worth, priorities, and perspective are of equal importance and relevance. Students will always question and challenge. The humanities program in Long Beach provides them with a framework of historical perspective within which to do that.

The course has grown to a full-year honors humanities class with 90 seniors and three instructors in a modified team. A one semester pilot academic "non-honors" humanities class was offered on an experimental basis during the 1969–70 school year. The humanities course is also offered now in four of Long Beach's five high schools.

Objectives — In addition to specific content objectives, which will be discussed later, the general objectives for the course are:

1. To offer students opportunities for enrichment in the humanities and the social sciences.
2. To encourage critical evaluation of ideas and issues.
3. To provide an intellectual environment that will help students to develop a better understanding of the relationship of humanities to other fields of learning.
4. To foster skills in critical thinking, critical reading, discussion, independent study, non-judgmental listening, and oral and written communication.
5. To ease the transition between high school and college through exposure to a variety of ideas and sources and through insistence on methods of exploration, analysis, and inquiry.

Organization and Staff — To qualify for supplemental state funds for the gifted, the honors humanities course is composed of two-thirds gifted and one-third academically talented students. A gifted student is one who ranks in the top 2 or 3 per cent on two out of three tests (intelligence, reading, math). An academically talented student usually ranks in the 100–125 IQ range with comparable reading scores. The pilot academic humanities course is designed to offer the content and method of the course to a wider number of students and is open to all academically talented students with no need to have two-thirds of the class made up of gifted students.

Honors humanities is a full-year course and meets the district's requirements for a year of social studies for seniors.

Academic humanities is a one-semester course and is offered for credit for the non-government semester of senior social studies. Because the readings and discussions often involve controversial issues, parents are asked to sign a consent slip to allow students to enroll in the class.

In honors humanities 90 students and three instructors meet in three separate rooms during one class period. Each instructor works in the area of his specialization: political philosophy, the arts, or man, society, and values. Each group spends 12 weeks with a single instructor and then moves on to a second and then to a third instructor for additional 12 week periods. A student's original group of 30 is changed at the end of 12 weeks so that he will not be with the same students during the entire year. Although the primary focus of instruction is with a single instructor and 30 students, there are a number of occasions when the entire group comes together for a common experience, such as a guest speaker or a field trip.

Academic humanities is a modified team of 60 students and two instructors. Political philosophy is not included, as students take a required semester of regular U.S. government. Each instructor takes a group of 30 students for nine weeks in his speciality (the arts or man, society, and values), and then the groups switch at the quarter. There are also opportunities for combined meetings.

The instructors have been social science or English teachers with extensive backgrounds in the humanities. At one time all three instructors had been year-long John Hay Fellows at either Columbia or Berkeley. Two of those instructors are now teaching at other schools in the district.

Course of Study — Although each instructor specializes in a given area, continual emphasis is placed on the interrelatedness of the areas. Art, as an example, has political overtones as society deals with questions of censorship and freedom of expression or as art and music express the feelings of a country. The study of ethics and morality whether of political man, artistic man, or whatever kind of man, provides a context and an interrelationship for the units.

Several questions are basic to the unit on man, society, and values: What is basis of value? What is the nature of man? What is the nature of ethics and morality? What is the relationship between society and man's search for values? What is the origin, purpose, and nature of society? What is the role of man as he relates to his society? What are some of the problems facing society today? What is the nature of the social sciences and what role do they play in reaching an understanding of man in society?

The unit is not organized chronologically, nor is it handled by time or cultural periods. The basic questions are dealt with as such by utilizing a variety of primary source readings ranging from the contemporary to the distant historical. Authors read during this unit include Emerson, Faulkner, Machiavelli, Augustine, Ortega y Gasset, Nietzsche, Joseph Wood Krutch, Oscar Wilde, Martin Buber, Reinhold Niebuhr, Cardinal Newman, Hume, and Carlyle.

The 12-week unit on the introduction to the arts is organized to help students understand the value of the arts in developing a fuller life, be acquainted with some of the major areas of controversy in the arts, know the major artistic movements of our time in the context of the past, become aware of elements of design, color, and harmony in their own lives, make discriminating aesthetic decisions, become more creative people, and include the enjoyment and understanding of the arts more broadly in their adult lives. Through reading, discussing, viewing, listening, and creating, students are exposed to contemporary issues, ideas, and expressions in the arts as well as receiving an introductory and historical survey of art from the Greeks to the 20th century.

The 12-week unit on political philosophy and government combines with six weeks of the unit on man, society, and values to meet the one-semester district requirement for a course in government. In addition to some of the prior questions about the origin, purpose, and nature of society, questions basic to this unit include: Is politics an art or science? How is political theory related to other disciplines? How is political theory related to society? How is political power related to the state? How is the problem of "Who should rule" resolved? What political institutions must man have? What are some of the major problems of democracy?

Attention is focused on the nature and purpose of local, state, and federal governmental structures. Emphasis on historical perspective is given and authors consulted — in addition to the traditional textbooks — include Plato, Aristotle, Hobbes, Locke, Montesquieu, Rousseau, and Burke.

The one-semester academic humanities class included the first two units mentioned above; each is reduced from 12 to 9 weeks and with an accompanying reduction in some of the readings.

Requirements — One major assignment is required in each 12-week unit — a creative project in the arts unit and a critique of a single book and a term paper for the other units. The creative project emphasizes a written analysis of the act of creation done by the student, not on a beautifully finished, professional product, although many of the projects (poetry, sculptures, paintings, musical compositions) are professional indeed. The student may choose the unit on which he wants to do his critique and his paper. He may criticize a book in political philosophy and write a paper on man, society, and values or he may do the reverse.

An additional assignment in the arts unit is keeping an aesthetic log in which students are expected to record and react to periodic exposures to experiences in the arts, such as museum trips, concerts, or plays.

Because of the heavy emphasis on primary reading and discussion, students are expected to take reading and discussion notes. Involvement in discussions as a participant and as a leader and occasional essay examinations are also part of the course requirements.

Activities — Much of the course is oriented around a seminar-discussion approach, using small groups as well as the basic group of 30 students. Speakers on issues relating to the course have come from the local state college and city college as well as from the community. Occasional field trips to places such as the Los Angeles County Art Museum, art galleries on La Cienega in Los Angeles, and plays at the Music Center in Los Angeles have taken place. Independent study is certainly another important activity of the course.

Probably one of the most important activities has been a spring weekend retreat to a mountain camp owned and used by the school district for its outdoor education program. This retreat began in the spring of 1963, again on the initiative of students, and has expanded to the other high schools in the district. From Friday afternoon through Sunday afternoon students are engaged in a rather exciting pursuit of ideas in an extension of classroom concerns and readings. The weekend is carefully planned by a student-faculty committee; a bibliography and theme are structured and disseminated several weeks prior to the weekend; outside speakers may provide additional stimulus; and small discussion groups, solitude, and some very significant fellowship are the focus of the weekend.

Materials — Multiple sources are used. Some titles are used in two or even three of the units, underscoring the interrelatedness of the units. All students work from the following books for one or more of the units: William Ebenstein's *Great Political Thinkers* (Holt), Milo Wold and Edmund Cykler's *An Introduction to Music and Art in the Western World* (Little, Brown), Paul Obler's *Mirrors of Man* (Van Nostrand-Reinhold), and Joseph Satin's *Ideas in Context* (Houghton Mifflin).

Students use outside sources for critiques, papers, and additional reading. By district policy, books must be selected from the high school or the city college library or else be jointly approved by parents and instructor. A variety of films, filmstrips, prints, tape recordings, and records are available from the district audio-visual center to supplement the course.

Eugene E. Best
Voluntary, non-credit summer course open to all students, grades 9–12; inquiry methods; field trips and multi-media; also full-year elective for seniors; thematic structure; team-teaching and small-large group instruction; flexible scheduling.

History — The Northern Valley Regional High School at Demarest first developed its summer program in the humanities six years ago as part of its enrichment courses in a comprehensive, tuition-free summer school. Since that time the course has been taught by three instructors and has become the base for a full-year senior English course, which carries a Carnegie unit. This new course was first offered in 1969–70. For purposes of clarity, the summer course is described first.

Objectives of the Summer Humanities Course —
1. To establish the interrelatedness of literature, art, music, drama, dance, architecture, philosophy, and history as expressions of man's personality and spirit.
2. To demonstrate universals of human expression.
3. To see man in perspective of his planet, his limitations, and his aspirations.
4. To raise significant questions such as, "What is man and whither does he go?"

Approach — The course utilizes the inquiry mode. During the first days, students and the teacher develop a series of questions about man that they wish to explore. These vary from summer to summer. Some questions that have been asked are: Do the buildings man create reflect a philosophy of life as well as a life style? How much are modern films in debt to other visual arts? Is man essentially aggressive? What does it mean to be Apollonian, Dionysian, and Promethean? How can we define civilization? What is self-expression? Has the past any relevance? Once the questions have been raised, the class structures itself so that fruitful discussion and useful inquiry can be carried out. The group clearly understands that the questions are more important than the answers.

Students and Instructors — The course is open to all high school students (grades 9 through 12) without reservation. It is a purely voluntary, non-credit course.

The course has always been taught by individual teachers who have credentials in several disciplines. The criteria for selection have been wide reading, broad interests, varied experience, and good rapport with students. The instructor must become part of the inquiry group if the course is to work well. He is essentially a resource person.

Requirements — Enough reading to be able to contribute to class discussions is all that is asked of a student. However, students frequently contribute essays, works of art, and 8mm films to the class.

The class meets for two hours a day, six days a week for five weeks.

Resources and Activities — The school's extensive AV holdings and a film rental budget of $500 are supplemented by materials brought in by students. The students bear the total cost of field trips. The school library operates during the summer.

Students are encouraged to react to the pivotal questions with creative expression in any of the arts. These works are often the basis for further class discussions and later may be included in a literary magazine published by the creative writing class that meets during the summer.

The close proximity to New York City enables the group to take at least one field trip a week. For instance, the following trips were made in one summer: Shakespeare in the Park, *South Pacific* at New York State Theater, Lincoln Center, a rock concert in Central Park, jazz concert at the Museum of Modern Art, a ballet evening at the New Jersey Cultural Center at Holmdel, The Metropolitan Museum of Art, The Guggenheim Museum, The Whitney Museum, and The Museum of the City of New York.

Materials — The classroom is definitely multi-media oriented. It is equipped with 16mm sound projector, overhead projector, slide projector, tape recorder, and record player. A frequently changed exhibit of art prints covers most of the walls. During one summer the following were used:

Films: NY, NY, Neighbors, Nobody Waved Goodbye, Appalachian Spring (danced by Martha Graham), *A is for Architecture, Michelangelo, Giant for an Age,* and *Night and Fog.*
Records: St. Joan by Shaw, *Medea, The War Requiem, A History of Music* (RCA), and selected compositions from several periods, including hard rock.
Slides: 300 slides from the art department collection.
Art prints: A changing exhibit.
Books: Great Gatsby, Death of a Salesman, King Lear, The Zoo Story, and *Red Badge of Courage.* (The students and teacher build a reading list.)

Objectives of the Full-Year Program — Actually the humanities course offered in 1969–70 is the first stage of a program that includes the principles of team-teaching within the administrative structure of a large-small group instruction and flexible scheduling. Because changes in the school's physical plant will not be complete until September 1970, only team-teaching and modified large-group instruction can be used now. The course of study is extremely fluid, since the three teachers who are teaching it wish to experiment in both content and approach. Therefore, all statements below are tentative.

The objectives are exactly those of the summer program. However, it has also been decided that the course should offer frequent opportunities for students to develop skills in composition and oral discourse.

The course is organized on a thematic basis. Some tentative themes to be discussed are: "War — What Does It Accomplish?" "The Physical World — Man in It — Man of It," "The City As an Expression of Man," and "Art — Frivolity or Utility."

Students and Instructors — The course is open to all seniors, carries credit toward graduation, and satisfies the requirement for English IV. (It is one of 16 electives that do so.)

Three instructors teach the course in a modified team approach. Some large-group instruction is done. The course is team-planned, and in-school planning time has been arranged by the administration.

Requirements — A course of reading is set up by the team and the students. Students are required to demonstrate their knowledge and understanding of the readings by participation in class discussions and by writing essays and critiques. In addition, students are required to develop individual projects in cooperation with their instructors. The scope of the projects is unlimited, and creativity is encouraged. Term papers are neither sought nor forbidden.

The course meets four times a week for a full academic year.

Resources and Activities — The resources of the Instructional Materials Center, the various department resource centers, and the talents of instructors from the art, social sciences, and science departments are available. We also plan to make use of field trips and field work.

The activities for the first year of operation parallel those designed during the summer experiences. However, since we cannot ask students to pay for so many trips, it is unlikely that more than five out-of-school activities will be attempted. Instead we have arranged for in-school performances by the Theater of the Deaf, a ballet troup, a string ensemble, and a mime. We expect to conduct a film festival also.

Materials — The first unit, which may or may not be representative, includes *All Quiet on the Western Front, Night and Fog* (film), *The Persian Women,* and *Seven Days in May*. Specific titles and experiences will be chosen for individual groups, and only the large-group instruction will be aimed at the entire group of 166 students.

CRISPUS ATTUCKS HIGH SCHOOL, INDIANAPOLIS, IND.

Judith R. Waugh*

Interdisciplinary approach to history, literature, music, and art; team-taught; two semesters for academically able students; flexible syllabus; students report on outside-school cultural events and prepare original compositions.

History and Approach — Humanities at Crispus Attucks High School — now six years old — is a two-semester, team-taught course designed to encompass four areas or disciplines: history, literature, art, and music. It functions under the auspices of the English department and has no resources outside the school. The course is primarily designed for students with academic potential. Its approach is interdisciplinary, the purpose being to make the student aware of the fact that the fields of history, literature, art, and music are interrelated and interdependent. The student must realize that one subject cannot really be isolated but should be considered in relation to other areas as integral parts of a whole. After some fundamental training, he soon learns to make associations and to recognize the common denominators.

Course of Study — The syllabus has been revised numerous times; last year it focused on revolutionary trends and new frontiers from mid-19th century to the present. The teachers found this period to be a dynamic and challenging one to

---

* EDITOR'S NOTE: Miss Waugh is now at John Marshall High School in Indianapolis.

teach, and explored, in the first semester, material ranging from the *Communist Manifesto*, Freud, Gompers, Ibsen, and Whitman, to Wagner, the Impressionists, and Frank Lloyd Wright. The first semester began with an in-depth study of the romantic movement as a revolt against classicism and concluded with a study of the socio-political milieu that existed at the time of World War I. The second semester continued with a study of the post-World War I period and culminated with a unit on modern protest from politics to jazz.

Requirements — All students are expected to hand in brief reports on cultural events they have attended outside of school. Nine reports are required each semester. In addition, students are required to participate in one debate or symposium during the year and to submit some individual project or prepare an original composition within one of the four disciplines.

Activities — Special activities can be informative and entertaining. They may range from a guest lecture on art nouveau to a folk sing with a guitarist; from an architectural tour to attending a play, concert, or ballet; from a student symposium to a debate. It is through experiences such as these that the student perceives the influence of one art upon another and acquires respect for artistic forms as well as the creative imaginations that produce them.

Discussions based on readings, lectures, films, slides, and current socio-political events and trends make up the bulk of class activity. The course is enlightening and fascinating to the student because of the broad areas of knowledge with which he becomes familiar and because he can (and is actively encouraged to) freely exchange ideas with others. Regular procedure allows for a flexible, challenging situation and a pleasant atmosphere. Through exposure, the student becomes more sophisticated, cultivated, and mature in his tastes, attitudes, and ideas — indeed, more aware of the importance of the humanities in his daily life.

Readings — During the two semesters the student is enrolled in humanities, he reads the whole or excerpts from the following: *Communist Manifesto,* "The Hero," "The Creative Process," "The Romantic Prophet," selected poems by Wordsworth, Shelley, Poe, Coleridge, Baudelaire, Mallarme, Verlaine, and Whitman, "Psychoanalysis and Man's Sense of His Own Importance," *The Interpretation of Dreams, Beyond Good and Evil, Origin of the Species,* William James' theories of pragmatism and religious existentialism, *A Doll's House, Ghosts, The Red Badge of Courage, The Jungle* and/ or *The Octopus,* Keyboard Jr. pamphlets ranging from Romanticism to freedom in the arts, *Only Yesterday, The Great Gatsby,* selected poems by Frost, Dos Passos, and e. e. cummings, *Native Son, The Stranger, Death of a Salesman, The Lonely Crowd, The Organization Man, The Fire Next Time,* "The City as Center and Symbol," "The City is the People," "Suburbia in Excelsis," *The Uses of the Past,* "Man as His Own Maker," and "The Self and Its Search for Ultimate Meaning."

Conclusion — A total awareness of the value of a humanities course is not always immediate; as a matter of fact, it may be six months, a year, or perhaps two years before the student realizes the advantages of having been liberated from compartmentalized education.

Perhaps the "most beautiful" and certainly the most important aspect of such a course as humanities is that everyone has something to give, and we (teachers included) are all richer human beings after association and interaction with and reaction to each other.

Dean S. Northrop

Structured around units on music, painting and sculpture, dance, opera, poetry, drama, and architecture; selected seniors experiment with and participate in all art forms; modified team-teaching; field trips and multi-media; individual creative projects replace final exam.

History and Objectives — The F. D. Roosevelt humanities program was initiated in 1961 as a full-credit course whose basic purpose was to introduce the seven fine arts to a select group of twelfth-grade students. It has continued to function with this approach, having the following aims:

1. To expose the student to all seven fine arts.
2. To enrich the esthetic range and depth of each student in the course.
3. To acquaint him with the great names and works in the seven fine arts.
4. To provide first-hand experience involving original art through field trips.
5. To increase his skills in articulating his impressions and reactions to art works.
6. To provide avenues of artistic expression for each individual in these art forms.

Approach and Course of Study — Except for the introductory three-week period and terminating projects, the course is broken up into units concentrating on specific art forms. A student has the following classes during the course of a year: music — six weeks; art (painting and sculpture) — six weeks; dance — two weeks; opera — three weeks; poetry

— three weeks; drama — three weeks; architecture — three weeks.

In the art unit, for instance, a student starts by actual work with paint to express feelings and moods. Through subsequent discussions, he becomes acquainted with the elements of painting and begins to apply them in his later experiments. Slides and prints are used extensively so the student can observe the techniques of great artists and learn to enjoy a wide range of artistic creations. The climax of the art unit is visits to three New York museums and a first-hand encounter with acknowledged masterpieces. Later in the course, each student has an opportunity to explore this medium further in an individual project if he so desires.

The drama unit, involving a performing art, contains discussions centering around the functions, purposes, and techniques of drama, followed by actual experimental work on stage using original or established works. Here every student is expected to participate in actual performances (informal and without an outside audience) and to explore the medium with as imaginative and unusual an approach as he wishes. Needless to say, this does not always produce dynamic or workable theater, but throughout the course each student is encouraged to experiment and create so that he may fully appreciate the potentialities, the limitations, and the sensory — emotional — intellectual appeals of each art form.

While there is some attempt to develop critical judgment of the various art media, it has been the experience of the staff that the units are too short and the student exposure to the media too brief to expect valid or significant student value judgments. At this point in his development, open-mindedness and willingness to explore all facets of the art are regarded as more desirable.

Students and Instructors — The course is composed of a select group of approximately 40 grade twelve students. Classes are usually divided into two equal groups for most units of study. Class members are selected by the guidance department, and the final screening is done by the humanities staff. While past academic achievement is a key factor, final selection is determined by a student's interest and his course of study. Those with science majors or whose past heavy schedules have necessitated by-passing the arts seem to profit especially from this course.

Three full-time teachers are scheduled for this one period. The art teacher handles painting, sculpture, and architecture units, while the music teacher covers the music and opera units. An English teacher teaches the poetry and drama units, and the dance unit is covered through films and an outside dancer consultant. All three staff members are scheduled for both the humanities class period and the conference period that follows. Thus each teacher is either teaching during the humanities period or is free to work on advance planning or has a free period for staff meetings and conferences. Some team-teaching is involved, especially in the introductory weeks and in the projects period.

Requirements — In addition to the actual exploration of the materials in each media, each student is expected to pursue certain studies in each unit. In architecture, each student explores a particular period, which he then presents through slides and a lecture to the class. In drama small committees can present to the class their findings on anything from what comprises a tragedy to the traits of the theater of the absurd.

Field trips are regarded as the laboratory for the course, and student are required to attend the trips to three art museums, a philharmonic concert, an opera, and an architectural tour of New York. In addition they are expected to attend local dance and dramatic productions as their lab for these art media. It is felt that this first-hand experiencing of art forms is essential to the realization of the course's objectives, and so careful advance classroom preparation is made to ascertain that each trip will be aesthetically, emotionally, and intellectually stimulating to each student. A written report is required after each trip as a means of observing exactly what new appreciations and understandings are developing.

Tests are given at the end of each unit. As the purpose of the course is greater aesthetic awareness and appreciation, these tests are not weighted very heavily but are aimed at checking the student's knowledge of the great artists and works in that medium as well as his growth in some critical judgment of quality art.

The full-year course, which meets four times a week, terminates in a series of projects, some individual and some group. An opportunity is provided for each student to explore in depth any particular art form that has attracted his special attention during the year. A typical set of projects might involve designing and producing some original rugs, an original folk music presentation, an on-stage happening, or an experimental original poetry presentation with music, lights, and projections. There is no final examination; the projects replace it as the terminating feature of the class.

Materials — The textbook *The Humanities* by Dudley and Faricy (New York: McGraw-Hill, 1967), art materials, film rentals on dance, library reference materials on humanities, fairly extensive collections of prints and slides, recordings, and community resources for musical and dramatic productions are utilized in the program.

The course is largely activity-oriented, concentrating on direct contact with both the materials of each art medium and original art works. Testing is kept to a minimum, and the staff concentrates on direct exposure to the art forms rather than much vicarious reading and writing about the mediums. The real criteria for judging the success of such an approach is the carry-over of student interest and appreciation after graduation; to judge from the reactions and comments of graduates, this particular course has proven one of the most stimulating and rewarding.

Dorothy Miles

One-semester "Man in Conflict" course for non-academic seniors; chronological and ideological study of the forces that have impelled Americans into armed combat; read historical novels, poems, and essays about the various wars; multi-media and field trips.

Objectives — Our "Man in Conflict" unit attempts a multi-media approach to the American heritage by a chronological and ideological study of the major social and environmental forces that have led Americans into armed combat, i.e., the American Revolution, the Civil War, World Wars I and II, Korea, and Vietnam. The unit is not designed to bombard students with a daily barrage of anti-war propaganda or to repudiate the facts of American history; rather it is designed to increase their understanding of what is meant by "our American heritage."

Various and conflicting points of view on the vital issues of each period are presented to enable each pupil to arrive at some conclusions *on his own* regarding (1) the relationship between conflict and the nature of man and (2) why Americans at several periods of crisis in their history have, through factors of either the emotion or factual environment, been impelled to armed conflict. The ultimate goal of the course is to have each pupil ask and attempt to answer *for himself* the following questions: Is war an inevitable social cataclysm? Is the choice always one between war and peace? In the past, what has armed conflict solved or not solved? With the acquisition of nuclear weapons by the major powers of the world shortly after World War II, what problems can be settled now or in the future by armed combat? What new conflict involving all Americans appears to be shaping, and by what means can it be resolved without resort to armed combat?

Approach and Students — "Man in Conflict" is a one-semester humanities unit created in 1966 at Marblehead High School for twelfth-grade general students and structured within the framework of a traditional three-year high school program. In 1971 Marblehead will convert from a conventionally structured English curriculum to an entirely new student-oriented, ungraded English program at which time the "Man in Conflict" unit will be offered to all interested pupils in their tenth, eleventh, or twelfth years on an optional basis and on two different achievement levels. As in the original course, the first level will be directed to non-academic pupils; the second will be directed to the average and the above-average pupils and will require more in-depth and independent study.

The course is adapted for use in our traditional building facility (vintage 1930) and is administered by the combined efforts of the English Department Chairman and two English instructors, who were chosen to teach the humanities unit because of their interest in American history as well as in American literature.

Course of Study — The course begins with the study of 18th century America, the rise of the revolutionary spirit, and the establishment of a democratic form of government. It proceeds to focus on the issues leading to each of our major wars and the end results, for example, the Civil War and the abolition of slavery and World War II and the elimination of Nazism. It concludes with a consideration of the conflict in Vietnam and the contemporary conflict over civil rights.

One historical novel of human involvement in each of the major wars is read as a basis for class discussion, for example, *Gone With the Wind, Hiroshima, The Bridge Over the River Kwai,* and *The Green Berets.* Each student is also required to pick from a list of selected readings one additional historical novel and a few poems and essays covering a specific period of his own choice. A large classroom library of paperbacks is kept for the independent reading assignments, which are geared to a variety of tastes and achievement levels. The reading materials reflect a wide range of expected achievement levels, all the way from Esther Forbes' *Johnny Tremain* to Jones' *From Here to Eternity* or Mailer's *The Naked and the Dead* or from Hardy's "The Man He Killed" to Aristophanes' *Lysistrata.*

Resources and Materials — Once the flavor of each distinct period of war or conflict has been tasted through the reading and the class discussions, recordings of the oratory of the day, which serve to better clarify and define the major issues of the conflict, are introduced along with period war songs and ballads. Lectures on the art and architecture of each historical period and occasional modern anti-war films are interspersed throughout the study of each period and often juxtaposed. The lectures are provided by the Museum of Fine Arts in Boston.

In addition to a large classroom library of paperbacks, a variety of records, tapes, and films have been assembled for the course. Wide use is made of our wealth of local history. Students are taken to view our famous painting, *The Spirit of '76,* and artifacts from personal collections of local families, particularly from the families of students, are solicited for lectures and displays. Field trips are planned to the local historical museums, and each class is taken to the theater to view *Gone With the Wind*, or, if they prefer, some other film germane to the theme of the unit. Musically inclined students are encouraged to involve themselves in the music of each period by preparing tapes of their own recordings or presenting period music "live" to the class; art students and photographers are encouraged to express themselves, through their own creative forms, on the major themes of man in conflict.

Nancy Moore

Required two-semester courses for ninth and tenth grades; both interdisciplinary, team-taught, value-oriented, flexible grouping, and multi-media; separate humanities department; daily three-period time blocks; humanities 9 organized around six units on cultural past and heritage; humanities 10 has six thematic units emphasizing modern man; CCTV facilities.

History — At present all students in grades nine and ten at Dobbs Ferry High School are humanities students. School year 1969–70 is the fifth year for humanities in the ninth grade and the second year for humanities in the tenth grade. It is also a year of increased correlation and emphasis on the humanities in grades eleven and twelve, with preparatory to full-scale courses offered on those levels.

Dobbs Ferry began its humanities program in 1965 and received a Title III grant in 1966 for the purchase of CCTV facilities, projectors, and printed materials. The humanities department is an entity in itself, although it works closely with related departments.

Objectives — The primary objective of the humanities program is the development of socially responsible, humane individuals. Other contributory objectives include:

1. Understanding of the meaning of the evolution of man and an appreciation of the place of the individual within this development.

2. Establishment of functional values within the individual and his understanding of their relationship to the values of others.
3. Ability to skillfully and effectively apply human resources to the orderly solving of problems.
4. Ability to integrate knowledge from divergent areas and apply it to an orderly search for truth.

Approach — Humanities 9 and 10 are both required two-semester, three-credit courses, replacing the former English and social studies curriculum. Both courses are interdisciplinary, team-taught, and value-oriented. In each case the teaching team of six represents the areas of English, social studies, art, and music, with additional strength in related disciplines such as philosophy, anthropology, psychology, and language. Each member of the teaching team is considered a humanities teacher first and the representative of an individual discipline second.

Course of Study — Humanities 9 is organized around six sequential units based primarily on cultural outlook. Unit 1 is a brief overview of the humanities and of contemporary man; Unit 2 centers on the nature and concerns of primitive man; Unit 3 studies classical Greece and China; Unit 4 studies the comparative views and cultures of medieval Europe, Hindu culture, and Islamic culture; Unit 5 deals with Renaissance Europe; and Unit 6 is a re-examination of contemporary man, his major problems, and the role of the humanities. Recurrent themes and chronology are part of this approach.

Humanities 10, designed to complement the ninth grade segment as well as to introduce the student to new approaches, is organized as a thematic sequence. The six units are: Unit 1, contemporary man; Unit 2, man's quest for dignity and freedom through an established order; Unit 3, man's quest for dignity and freedom through revolution; Unit 4, man's quest for identity in times of change;

Unit 5, man's quest for dignity and freedom through romantic vision and realistic method; and Unit 6, brave new world. Modern man is emphasized in this course.

Scheduling and Grouping — Students meet generally in a three-period time block each day. They are regrouped for each unit of the course, and a new schedule is made up by the teaching team to fit the needs of each week and unit.

In discussion before the start of each unit, the team determines what kinds of groups should exist in terms of unit objectives and observations of student needs and behavior. In some instances students are given a choice of several different kinds of grouping. At other times group assignments are made by the team. Each unit brings opportunities for new kinds of group membership and new experiences. Students fully understand this and find the prospect of this kind of change every six weeks or so quite refreshing.

A number of different types of student grouping that have been tried successfully in Humanities 9 and 10 are:

1. Independent study — individual project and paper required, student released from regular classes, attends teacher conferences regularly.
2. Literary seminar — emphasis on literary analysis for advanced students.
3. Photography group — students make own exhibits and films based on unit themes.
4. TV group — students of mixed abilities design and produce an original video-tape as a three-week project, based on unit themes.
5. Debating teams — students debate current issues.
6. Work teams — small groups of three to five students pursue unit objectives with teachers as resource persons, emphasis on discovery and sharing of responsibility; group audio-visual report required.
7. Remedial groups — classes of ten to twelve students con-

centrate on improving reading and writing skills; work based on unit objectives and themes.

8. Newspaper or magazine staff — four to five students publish news of students' work in the humanities; grade nine publishes a newspaper, grade ten publishes a magazine.

9. Dance group — students present work related to unit themes and objectives.

10. Drama group — students, selected for interest, present work related to unit to other students;

11. Supervised study — teacher-directed classroom work, closely guided, for students needing close supervision and much structure.

To minimize labeling certain students, humanities groups are always named for famous persons, concepts, or movements relevant to each unit.

Naturally grouping has a direct influence on scheduling. For each group, a program of activities is designed to aid in reaching unit objectives. No two groups will necessarily carry out the same activities or follow a similar schedule within the same unit. Some groups will rotate among five or six different teachers; others will not. A common core of material is presented each day in large-group instruction, where 120–140 students (one entire grade) meet as a class for films, slide analysis, group singing, concerts, and other activities. Students are given a new schedule each week; designing this schedule is one of the tasks (and freedoms!) of the teaching team.

Activities and Requirements — Student activities are the most essential item in the humanities courses, since the student's experiences *are* his education. Activities are designed to lead the student toward attainment of specific unit objectives, stated in terms of understandings and appreciations. Discovery of relationships and creative, disciplined expression are emphasized. Many individual assignments cut across discipline lines. In addition to analytical, interpretive, and reaction papers, students frequently are assigned problems calling for solutions in graphics or other media. In the course of their study of the humanities, students listen to records, tapes, and other students; they look at films, filmstrips, and slides; they carry out library research and interview resource people; they form instrumental and vocal groups and give performances for other students; they give their own large-group presentations, featuring student demonstrations, audience participation, and student-made filmstrips; they visit museums and theaters on class and individual field trips; they learn to use film and overhead projectors, microphones, and CCTV equipment; they create collages, sketches, models, cartoons, mobiles, mosaics, paintings, "stained glass windows," sculptures, and music. They work individually and in groups of great variety, with and without closely defined structure. A detailed listing of activities for each unit in Humanities 9 is available in the course of study, which may be purchased from the Dobbs Ferry Humanities Department. The Humanities 10 course of study is currently being prepared.

Film Study Series and Materials — Humanities 9 and Humanities 10 each present a film series designed to increase students' appreciation of this art form. The series runs throughout the year and features a variety of film types from foreign and domestic sources. Highly successful films include: *La Strada, Nobody Waved Goodbye, Bridge Over the River Kwai, The Golden Fish, Citizen Kane, High Noon, The Treasure of the Sierra Madre, Nothing But a Man, The Shop on Main Street, The Red Balloon, The Gold Rush,* and *Billy Budd.* Worksheets and discussions accompany the analysis of each film.

Both Humanities 9 and Humanities 10 have separate materials centers adjacent to team meeting rooms and equipment centers. In addition the high school library maintains an increasingly effective collection of humanities materials. At present bound collections of excerpts and worksheets exceed 100 pages for each unit of Humanities 9, and the Humanities 10 collections are of similar proportions. Seven general literature and social science texts are supplemented by a great quantity of paperbound and hard cover resources, including many contemporary novels.

Helen G. Severs

Twelfth-year English students of all ability levels study the literature, drama, poetry, art, architecture, and music of five thematic-cultural eras; flexible, changing approach, content, and requirements; student involvement in arts and discussions encouraged; multimedia resources.

Rationale and General Description — The content of the course, the manner of presentation, and the related activities differ from year to year, as do the groups of twelfth-year students of English who participate. This number includes students of every level of ability; however, requirements vary according to interest and skills. For example, research is of two types — the report and the thesis. Within the same group, one student might discover the main features of Gothic architecture and give his finding orally to the class; another might study the character and tale of Chaucer's Pardoner and show his sincerity or insincerity in a sermon.

Opportunities to attend a performance of a play being studied, visit an art museum, see a one-man art exhibit, hear a visiting lecturer, artist, or philosopher, hear a madrigal or instrumental ensemble, entertain the regional ballet director-lecturer with his troupe of performers, or listen to a Bible scholar lecture have all, at times, added much to the program. These events are interspersed in the course where they are relevant.

Direct student involvement is possible through the composition or performance of music, presentation of reports on architecture, artists, or representative figures, and similar topics, acting, reading, or discussing literary and drama selections, creating paintings, sculpture, masks, costumes, stage background, or dances.

Recently evolving is a student-action project, which links the student with some service to the family, school, community, or the larger world. Reading and discussion of current books and major periodicals, e.g., *The Saturday Review, The New Republic, Schools Without Failures,* and the *World As Teacher,* precede these projects.

Approach — The approach varies from studying background materials to immediate involvement in a play, a musical composition, or a work of art, according to student-leader circumstances. Thus at one time, study of Edith Hamilton's *Mythology* and *The Greek Way,* the *Horizon Book of Ancient Greece,* and water colors, sketches, and photographs of buildings and sculpture of Greece might precede the reading of, say, *Antigone*; at another time the reading of the play or a consideration of the Acropolis might be more effective with the supporting materials studied later.

Resources — Immediacy, variety, and sensuous appeal are achieved by showing slides from several collections. Recordings of readings, ballads, plays, and music enliven the literary and musical portions of the program. Excellent films, such as *Meaning in Modern Painting, Chartres Cathedral, Arts of the Middle Ages* by John Canaday, *Marc Chagall* by Vincent Price, *Steps of the Ballet, The Ageless Mozart* by Leonard Bernstein, and *Plato's Apology, The Red Balloon, A Doll House,* and *The Cherry Orchard,* supply visual variety. Good-sized prints of paintings, photographs of sculpture and architecture, original sculpture, and reproductions well displayed in the classroom cultivate appreciation and informal discussion. References to Klee, Wyeth, and Picasso happen naturally when copies of their works are daily in sight.

Understanding, appreciation, and enjoyment of other cultures and views of life with the ultimate enrichment of the student's own, is the objective of the humanities program.

Course of Study for "The Measure of Man"

Unit 1, Through Psychological Insights and Self-Realization: In the Modern Western World. The individual rather than in the universal is emphasized. Characteristics are: the personal, subjectivity, tonal quality, mood, emotion, change, inner reality, abstraction, symbols, and the mystical.

Readings: From Camus, Paton, Eliot, D. H. Lawrence, Dreiser, Joyce, Dostoyevsky, Mansfield, Porter, Kafka, Conrad, Unamuno, Sartre, Beckett, Dylan Thomas, Henry Reed, Spender, Auden, Yeats, C. Day Lewis, Betjeman, A. Huxley, Forster, Wilfred Owen, Moore, cummings, Roethke, Flaubert, A. Miller, Chekhov, Faulkner, Crane, Woolf, O'Neill, Ibsen, Heller, and Sholokov may be used.

Specific suggestions include: *Too Late the Phalarope,* "The Grand Inquisitor," *The Heart of Darkness, The Lagoon,* "Fern Hill," "The Wind Blows," *The Dubliners, The Stranger,* "The Hollow Men," *Ship of Fools,* "The Hunger Artist," "The Naming of Parts," *Waiting for Godot,* "The Rocking Horse Winner," *Sons and Lovers,* "Dulce et Decorum Est," "The Wild Swans at Coole," "Winter Landscape," *Catch 22, The First Circle,* "Metamorphosis," "Lessons of War: Naming of Parts," "Bombers," "Masee de Beaux Arts," *No Exit, The Hairy Ape, Madame Bovary, The Death of a Salesman,* and current periodicals.

Art: Moore's *Reclining Figure,* Miro's *Figure 103,* Seurat's *La Grande Jatte,* Ryder's *The Race Track,* DeChirico's *Melancholy and Mystery of a Street,* Calder's *Lobster Trap and Fish Tails,* Munch's *The Scream,* Picasso's *Guernica, Ma Jolie,* and *Don Quixote,* Klee's *With the Two Lonely Ones,*

Hassam's *Church at Old Lyme*, Rodin's *Balzac*, Brancusis's *Bird in Space*, Wyeth's *Christina's World*, Hooper's *Early Sunday Morning*, Cezanne's *Still Life with Apples*, Van Gogh's *Starry Night*, Duchamps' *Nude Descending the Staircase*, Chagall's *I and My Village*, and Tcheltichev's *Hide and Seek*.

Architecture: Wright, Saarinen, Van Der Rohe, Le Corbusier, and the UN Building.

Music: Debussy's *La Mer*, Nocturnes and Preludes, Ravel's *Pavanne* and *Bolero*, Falla's *Nights in the Gardens of Spain*, Schonberg's Piano Pieces Op. 11, 25, and Mahler's Symphony No. 1.

Films: New Ways of Seeing (Roger Tilton), *Meaning in Modern Painting, Marc Chagall* by Vincent Price, *Ruth St. Denis and Ted Shawn* (interview and three performances: "Incense," "White Nautch," "Japanese Warrior") *Steps of the Ballet, Marcel Duchamps, The Cherry Orchard,* and *A Doll House.*

Unit 2, Through Reason: In Classical Greece and the Neo-Classical Western World. The interest is in the universal rather than in the individual. Characteristics are: reason, form, rules, order, edification, intellect, restraint, noble ideas, and dignified language.

Readings: From Homer, Aeschylus, Sophocles, Euripedes, Aristophanes, Plato, Aristotle, Moliere, Racine, Voltaire, La Fontaine, Swift, Pope, Jonson, Milton, Arnold, Eliot, and the Bible may be used.

Specific suggestions include: *The Illiad, Oedipus Rex, Agamemnon, Antigone, The Republic,* "The Nature of Tragedy," *The Birds,* "The Apology," The Genesis Creation, *The Would-Be Gentleman,* "L'Allegro" and "Il Penseroso," "Hymn to Diana," portions of *Paradise Lost, Gulliver's Travels, An Essay on Criticism, Murder in the Cathedral, Candide,* and *Prometheus Bound.*

Art: The Parthenon and friezes from it, Mount Vernon, The Pantheon, Palazzo Farnese, Monticello, Arc de Triomphe, *Hermes* by Praxiteles, *The Death of St. Francis* by Giotto,

Bacchus by DaVinci, *Oath of the Horatii* by David, *Adoration of the Magi* by Durer, *Madonna della Sedia* and *School of Athens* by Raphael, bust of Brutus by Michelangelo, Hogarth's *The Rake's Progress*, and DaVinci's *The Last Supper*.

Music: The symphony, the sonata, the concerto: Beethoven's Symphony No. 4 in B Flat Major, Op. 60, Mozart's Symphony in D Major, K 385 and Sonata in F Major, K 332, Prokofiev's Classical Symphony in D Major, Bach's Preludes and Fugues from the "Well-Tempered Clavichord," and Bloch's Concerto Grosso for Piano and String Orchestra.

Films: World History: An Overview (Man's Needs), *The Age of Sophocles, Man and God, Oedipus* (series), *Athens: The Golden Age, Plato's Apology* (Life and teachings of Socrates), *Aristotle's Ethics* (Theory of Happiness), *The Ageless Mozart* by Leonard Bernstein, and *Leonard Bernstein and the N.Y. Philharmonic in Berlin* (symphonies).

Unit 3, Through Faith: In Medieval England and Western Europe. The ideal is an earthly life so lived as to assure eternal bliss. The convention of chivalry idealized the devotion to God, lord, and lady. Devotional and pietistic works in literature and art and acts such as pilgrimages and crusades contrast with the bold naturalism of earthier elements within themselves and in such separate forms as the fabliaux.

Readings may include: ballads; the mystery plays of *Abraham and Isaac, The Deluge,* and the *Second Shepherds' Play*; Malory's *Morte d'Arthur*; "Aucassin and Nicolette," Chaucer's *Canterbury Tales*, especially the "Prologue," "The Pardoner's Tale," "The Prioress Tale," and "The Nun's Priest's Tale"; Eliot's *Murder in the Cathedral*; *Sir Gawain and the Green Knight*; and *The Once and Future King*.

Art: The general plan, scope, and significance of the Gothic cathedral: Chartres — its special features of construction, buttresses, spires, rose windows, sculpture, carvings, and stained glass; slides of illuminations and miniatures from medieval manuscripts (from a collection of slides photographed at Bodleian, Oxford).

Music: Gregorian chant, the ballad, medieval instruments, especially the lute, minstrels and mistrelsy, and medieval notation.

Films: Chartres Cathedral, The Meaning of Feudalism, The Medieval World, Arts of the Middle Ages by John Canaday and *Three Paintings of Hieronymous Bosch.*

The final two units, which follow a similar pattern, are: Unit 4, Through Experience: In Renaissance England and Italy; and Unit 5, Through the Exercise of Emotion and Freedom: In Romantic Victorian England and the Western World.

Eula Gayl Cutt
Four elective semesters of "Latin Heritage" to give inner-city, educationally deprived students a knowledge and appreciation of the Graeco-Roman world; under aegis of foreign language department; Latin is not taught in traditional fashion but used to strengthen English language skills; multi-media materials; some team-teaching.

History and Objectives — In September 1964, an experimental course, "Latin Heritage," was instituted at Northwestern High School. In September 1968, at the constant request of students, a second year was added to the program. Most students at Northwestern do not study a language. In fact, many counselors do not recommend it. The regular language courses spell failure. Since Northwestern is an inner-city school, many of the students come from educationally deprived backgrounds, which do not give them an opportunity to achieve academically, especially where success depends on language skills.

Since the heritage of the Graeco-Roman world is so rich, students are unaware that they encounter it every day. Every child should learn about, know, and feel that he is a part of this rich heritage; this enrichment should not be just experienced by the privileged few. The chief goals of this course are:

1. To develop the student's sense of achievement.
2. To know some success in the academic sphere.
3. To enrich his knowledge of the Graeco-Roman world and heritage.

4. To strengthen skills in his own language.
5. To express his talents, often latent.
6. To experience the enjoyment of manipulating a foreign language.
7. To prepare for further foreign language study.

Approach and Requirements — There are no definite measurable skills that students must attain. That depends on the class. The teacher attempts to achieve the general objectives that have been set forth. However, there are some general concepts that the student will learn: man's interpretation of the world outside himself; an understanding of democracy and the constant struggle for developing as an individual; the heritage and vestige of the past in his environment; and the universal verities of man's behavior. Outside reading and other activities offer the more gifted student opportunities. There is a great potential in allowing for individual differences.

Activities — Transparencies, art, and filmstrips are made by students. According to their interests and abilities, students do creative writing, both poetry and prose, publish a class magazine, and make puzzles, maps, derivative charts, clothing, and illustrated dictionaries, and so forth. They go to the museum and local theater.

Students and Instructors — The course is under the aegis of the foreign language department and is taught by Latin teachers who also have English majors. The teacher needs a wide range of knowledge of the ancient world, and a knowledge of Greek and ancient Greek culture is another great asset.

A student may take one semester or a complete two years. Most of the students are language handicapped. The class meets everyday. There is usually one section each semester, which is a control group, kept together in remedial reading and English, with the focus on Latin heritage. This involves team-teaching. Some students gain a skill in language so that they transfer at different levels to a traditional foreign language (Latin or modern language).

Course of Study

Latin: Study of the Latin language is emphasized to strengthen the student's skill in his own language and enrich his English vocabulary by learning derivatives, prefixes, suffixes, and common Latin phrases, abbreviations, and mottoes. He is introduced to oral Latin and learns vocabulary not often presented in a traditional Latin class, such as foods, colors, parts of the body, and conversational phrases and words. The teacher sets the goals according to students' abilities. Much of the fourth semester is devoted to reading Latin, particularly stories from mythology.

Mythology: Background material is stressed to impart not only a knowledge of mythology but also an awareness of it in the contemporary world. The mythology covered is given in two paperback texts.

Greek and Roman life and history: In the first semester Greek life and history are studied. These are some of the topics: Greek daily life (comparison and contrast to our culture), map study, concept of democracy, Socrates, Homer, Olympic games, and Hippocrates.

During the second semester, the focus is on Roman private life (comparison and contrast to our own culture), heritage from Rome, horoscopes, history of our calendar, and Julius Caesar.

In the third semester, some of the topics are: the constellations, astronomy, and the muses (introduction of a study of poetry in English).

The fourth semester is a continuation of Roman life and culture — Virgil, Horace, and so on.

A teacher could not possibly cover all topics. He is guided by his knowledge and the students' interests and abilities.

Materials and Resources — Books include Latin texts and paperback texts. During the first year *Gods, Heroes, and Men of Ancient Greece* by W. H. D. Rouse (Signet Key Book) is read and during the second year *Classical Mythology* by Edith Hamilton (Mentor Book).

Filmstrips, movies, slides, transparencies, records, art, pictures, maps, and TV programs are used extensively. The department of foreign language is assembling its own filmstrips, records, and transparencies. The Detroit public school audio-visual library and Detroit public library furnish much material. Libraries and paperbacks provide materials at students' reading levels. Much material must be prepared by the teacher.

There is a very sketchy syllabus available for the first year program. However, with a grant furnished by the American Classical League, a complete curriculum guide is being written. It is hoped that it will be available in the near future.

THE EDUCATIONAL LABORATORY THEATRE
PROJECT, NEW ORLEANS, LA.

Shirley Trusty

Brings living theatre and classical literature to 10–12 grade students in public and parochial schools as part of English curriculum; study packets for teachers and principals and reading copies for students usually provided prior to each of four annual presentations; workshops, actors' visits, and theatre tours.

Rationale and Objectives — The Educational Laboratory Theatre Project, in conjunction with the Repertory Theatre, New Orleans, which is supported by federal grants under Titles III and IV of ESEA and by the National Endowment of the Arts, is a three-year program aimed at establishing a permanent theatre in New Orleans and bringing living theatre to secondary school students. The program exposes high school students to the direct impact of the living theatre and to the classic literature that is its foundation. It provides a means for improving today's curriculum and developing tomorrow's audiences, and offers high-quality theatre to the community at large. Its set of guidelines for the use of live theatre as an integral part of the high school curriculum should benefit school systems everywhere.

Approach — The plays are viewed as part of the English curriculum, and reading copies for each of the plays are provided to all 40,000 students. The only exceptions to this policy have been *Charley's Aunt*, the initial presentation, and the theatre of the absurd presentations by Eugene Ionesco, *The Chairs*, and *The Bald Soprano*.

Methodology, Schedules, and Students — The program is open to every tenth-, eleventh-, and twelfth-grade student in the public and parochial high school of the New Orleans metropolitan area — 40,000 students annually. Fifty-three high schools participate. Each school attends four plays annually. The plays are all scheduled during the school day, and students are bussed to and from the Civic Theater. Fifteen hundred students attend daily during the school year.

Content — The plays presented, in order of appearance, have been: first year — Brandon Thomas's *Charley's Aunt*, William Shakespeare's *Romeo and Juliet*, Thornton Wilder's *Our Town*, and Richard Brinsley Sheridan's *The Rivals*; second year — Arthur Miller's *The Crucible*, William Shakespeare's *A Midsummer Night's Dream*, George Bernard Shaw's *Saint Joan*, and (Jean Poquelin) Moliere's *Tartuffe* and third year — G. B. Shaw's *Arms and the Man*, William Shakespeare's *Twelfth Night*, Henrik Ibsen's *An Enemy of the People*, and Eugene Ionesco's *The Chairs* and *The Bald Soprano*.

Instructors — Study packets, which include the play, a study guide, suggested classroom activities, supplementary teaching aids, and visual displays, are sent to the 504 English and speech teachers in the program and to all school principals and administrators. A record and filmstrip have been developed as additional instructional tools. In-service sessions are scheduled for the teachers to explore the fullest potential for teaching each play and making the theatre experience a part of the total school curriculum.

A special summer experimental workshop, "Improvisation Techniques in the Teaching of Dramatic Literature," was held for English teachers during the second summer of the program. Development work in this teaching device has provided a basis for further research. The Educational Laboratory Theatre Project and the Central Midwestern Regional Education Laboratory in St. Louis cosponsored a national symposium on "Improvisation and the Teaching of English" during the third year of the program. Classroom development in this area continues.

Activities

Press Conferences: Four conferences are held annually for high school journalists with the full theatre company. Interviews and photography sessions are the orders of the day. Repertory theatre is meaningful news to the high school newspapers of the area, and school press coverage helps to establish a strong sense of identity between students and theatre.

Assembly Programs and Visits of Actors into the Schools: Visits of actors to the schools and special assembly programs play an important part in the program. A wide range of assembly programs have been presented by the acting company, such as "Shakespeare, the Dramatist," "Presentational versus Representational Theatre," "Conscience in Conflict;" and a series of scenes from various plays selected to provide new perspectives for viewing the major production of the company, *The Crucible*. Actors' visits to classrooms and to drama clubs for informal discussion periods have been very popular. There are approximately 50 visits by actors per school year to the classrooms.

A program, "Negro Poetry," presented by company member Joanna Featherstone, was particularly popular with the schools. Miss Featherstone's unique presentational manner included audience participation in many chants and refrains.

The third year program initiated a new approach to instruction with the creation of a special touring company and a script entitled "The Necessities — Preparing for Ionesco," it was presented to students before they encountered the main stage productions of Ionesco's *The Bald Soprano* and *The Chairs*. The show toured for a five-week period and played in auditoriums, gyms, and cafeterias.

Theatre Workshops for Drama Students: Four theatre workshop series are held annually during the school year for speech and drama students. All workshops take place at the theatre. The third-year program format is a typical one — Tony Montanaro and Michael Henry, outstanding mime artists, introduced the year's series with a program of pantomime followed by a student workshop session. The second series was conducted by Viola Spolin, author of *Improvisation for Theatre,* and featured student participation in theatre games. Technical theatre was the focus of the third program conducted by the professional theatre staff. Stuart Vaughan, producing director of the Repertory Theatre, concluded the third-year series with workshop sessions on directing.

Teacher Workshops for Drama Teachers: To provide opportunities for confrontation of educators and artists, teacher workshops for drama teachers were introduced during the third season. Mr. Montanaro conducted the opening teacher workshop on pantomime, followed by a series on improvisation by Miss Spolin. Mr. Vaughan concluded the series with sessions on directing.

Special Exhibits and Workshops: Workshops for art students, featuring scenic and costume design, have been held. All sessions have been conducted by members of the professional theatre staff. Student costumes and scenic designs for *The Rivals* were developed and exhibited in the foyer of the theatre. Exhibits by members of the university art departments have been held at the theatre in conjunction with the third-year program. Original student university art was done in conjunction with the Ionesco productions.

Tours of Theatre and Facilities: Many student groups have taken advantage of the opportunity to visit the costume and scene shops and to observe the theatre staff at work. Attendance at theatre rehearsals and tours of the backstage area have been other sources of student activity and interest.

Lucille G. Jordan
Humanities approach to all instruction being developed and applied throughout elementary and secondary systems; extensive in-service experiences for teachers; curriculum revisions for four-quarter, 12-month program; multi-media, role-playing, discussion, field trips, and use of community resources.

Rationale and History — For five years the Atlanta public schools have given constant attention to incorporating a humanities approach into all their instructional programs. This emphasis was a natural outgrowth of numerous factors: a summer humanities program that included a two-week educational tour for senior high school students; a Title III ESEA program in which instructional teams worked in the humanities; many teachers in Atlanta working in the humanities on an individual basis with little contact among themselves; a Ford and Danforth grant permitting one school to develop an extensive humanities program for a highly selected group of students from a low socio-economic community; a group of about 20 teachers and supervisors attending the Humanities Conference sponsored by NCTE in New York in May 1967; the opening of the Memorial Arts Center in Atlanta in October 1968; and a school administration interested in providing organizational leadership for humanities programs.

Stressing a positive approach, the initial thrust was made by a manageable sized group of teachers who had manifested an interest in offering a concentrated humanities experience to a group of senior high school students. Following three summer seminars for about 30 academically talented students, observed feedback prompted the teachers to include creative, searching, less studious youngsters as well, and they successfully enlarged the program by incorporating both groups during the summers of 1968 and 1969.

A Title III project set up several instructional teams during the 1965–69 academic years to integrate social science, language arts, art, music, and drama at both the elementary and secondary levels. As continuous in-service experiences were necessary for teachers working on these teams, many other teachers throughout the 157 school system became aware of the effects of this approach to teaching and asked that it be included in their in-service experiences.

Senior high school students were then approached through their teachers to identify and explore concerns important to their own decision-making needs as young citizens. Through the collaboration of an Atlanta community theater group and school personnel responsible for in-service and curriculum development plans, three presentations were created and taken to each of the 25 high schools. Teachers, theater personnel, and curriculum specialists were involved in writing the presentations and deciding on preparation and follow-up activities for these improvisational dramas, discussions, and role-playing sessions. Such an approach was in line with the philosophy and definition of the humanities expressed by the group of interested high school teachers, namely:

> The humanities is that which makes man more humane, more sensitive to himself, his fellowmen, and his world. Humanities instruction should provide an opportunity for students to synthesize knowledge, thus, avoiding a separation of disciplines.

Elementary teachers who joined the initial group of persons interested in the humanities approach to teaching needed opportunities to share ideas and materials among their diverse groups and at the same time be apprised of what was developing at the secondary level, not only as related to the drama tour, but how teachers of specific disciplines correlated subject areas, provided for individualized instruction, utilized all instructional media including community resources, and how they organized and evaluated what they were doing.

The Title III staff coordinated the activities of three groups of persons for these in-service meetings during 1967–69. These groups, meeting together at times and separately on other occasions, were: (1) elementary teachers engaged or interested in engaging in the humanities approach to teaching, (2) secondary teachers of subjects that correlate to form "core" humanities programs, and (3) secondary teachers of "pure" humanities programs.

The Atlanta system is entering the second year of a four-quarter, 12-month school year at the high school level. An elective course called the "Humanities" has been offered for credit since the rewriting of the total secondary curriculum. Greater flexibility in scheduling in the new curriculum offerings has provided opportunities for integrating two or three subject areas into a large time-block, making possible an alternative way of presenting humanities experiences. A revision of the total elementary curriculum is underway in preparation for the movement of the 117 elementary schools to the four-quarter, 12-month program.

No doubt, we would all agree that interdisciplinary humanities activities that help pupils to look, listen, feel, and express themselves creatively and individually should be built in to every school program from pre-school through graduate school. However, unless an administrative group responsible for curriculum revision emphasizes this philosophy, learning becomes textbookish, fragmented, externalized, fact-oriented and "all branches but no roots." Fortunately, the Atlanta superintendent, Dr. John Letson, a member of the Arts and Humanities Foundation, has provided such direction in his declaration that education in the Atlanta system must develop in all students responsiveness as well as responsibility as individual citizens.

Objectives — The resource units which were developed by groups of teachers and from which teaching units were pulled according to their diagnosis and prescription of pupil needs, run the gamut of the chronological, thematic, biographical, moralistic, psychological, and political approaches.

The objectives of the wide variety of programs have been generally agreed upon as:

1. To teach pride in the diverse roots that make up the tapestry of human history, thus providing students from various backgrounds with appreciation for the contributions of *all* men to these accomplishments.
2. To heed the call of present social unrest and to provide experiences for open, critical thinking, and understanding of the decision-making process for individuals and groups.
3. To structure curriculum and teaching styles to get inside the "tuned off" student and to heed his urgent plea for relevance.
4. To find many ways to ignite the thrill of learning and to see that students are shielded from the fear of failure.
5. To break away from traditional ways of presenting subject matter by attempting new, alternative presentations.
6. To find keys that unlock the creative potential of students and lead them to use their intelligence and talents with confidence in attaining their goals.
7. To create an open classroom atmosphere by easing the pressures of competition with others and instead stressing the discovery of self-potential.
8. To develop characteristics of the *humane* individual as evidenced by each student and teacher respecting the dignity of each person at all times.

Schedules

High school: summer seminar, 8:30–12:00 daily for eight weeks, 5 hours credit.

High school: regular quarter in school year, a two-hour block of time daily, 5 hours credit.

Elementary school: built into regular school program, integrating all subject areas according to ingenuity of the teacher or teachers.

Activities — The multi-media approach, the conscious overlapping of several stimuli to produce total environment and new meanings, was one of the most effective experimental techniques. With a semi-darkened room, narration, and appropriate music and sound effects, students were immersed in complete environment and felt that they were experiencing life around them. Such an approach is effective in creating a panorama of historical incidents and helping students to perceive in totality and to make meaningful comparisons.

A familiar song like "Sitting on the Dock of the Bay" was juxtapositioned with a poem like Longfellow's "The Tide Rises and The Tide Falls" to create new meanings. Plaintive pictures, clipped from current magazines and interspersed with art from the ages, were stapled together in a long horizontal roll and pulled through the opaque projector to the strains of a song like "Sounds of Silence" to depict man's eternal mood of loneliness. By mixing in the self-identifying materials of the students themselves, it is easier to establish a beachhead of communication with alienated youth. Such an experimental environment is invaluable for reaching the "gut-level," as one educates by means of the emotions as well as the intellect.

Another significant technique is role-playing and dramatization. Adolescents cry for creative self-expression, and self-realization can be achieved only if creative imagination is given full play. A hodgepodge of activities served smorgasbord fashion was sometimes most productive in understandings, for instance a discussion comparing key scenes dramatized from *Romeo and Juliet* and *West Side Story*. Role-playing and dramatization provide wholesome outlets for pent-up emotions, help youngsters overcome self-consciousness, and aid them in improving oral and bodily expression. There is the added bonus that, by working together, understanding of self and others develops as does a keen interest in the ways human beings solve their problems. When young people are given leeway to develop their own learning experiences, they take responsibility spontaneously with great enthusiasm and emotion.

Another popular, though not unique, procedure used is discussion; two or more in small groups or large-group discussions are especially planned. Reading assignments for low-ability students are short. Higher-ability students do special in-depth studies and bring findings to the class for reactions. There are usually no right and wrong answers. Students are given every opportunity to clarify their values in relation to their own set of experiences and those of others.

Study trips are an integral part of the humanities course. Community resources for all areas of instruction have been identified in a *Community Resources Directory* that was recently developed and placed in each school library. Human resources are brought into the schools, and classes or groups of students visit museums, galleries, places of interest, and performances related to a particular on-going study. To create an atmosphere conducive to creative writing, actual perceptual experiences are given as often as possible.

Materials — Persons involved in teaching by the humanities approach have shared lists of instructional materials they had found effective. A composite list was distributed to all persons in the in-service groups so that they might share materials, or if funds became available to purchase instructional aids, persons who had used them could be contacted for evaluation. Materials and equipment used include: books (paperbacks especially), reproductions of arts (prints), maps (literary and pictorial), world panorama of literature, magazines and pamphlets, records and record player, tape recorders and audio-tapes, listening stations (including earphones), movie projectors and short and full-length movies, filmstrip projectors with slide attachments, overhead projectors, opaque projectors, educational television programs, and especially planned radio programs using resource persons.

Conclusions — The humanities approach to teaching has not been objectively evaluated by formal research methods, but educators involved have made the following subjective observations:

For teachers and administrators:

1. Less emphasis on cognitive learning alone, with new ways viewed to develop thrusts in areas of aesthetic, sensory, and affective learning.
2. Opportunity to develop a multi-cultural curriculum, thus unifying interests of diversified classes.
3. Teacher's role changes as he realizes he is "off the spot" of having to plan and organize all learning opportunities. He relaxes and operates humanely with students developing self-direction and independence.
4. Teachers dealing with many broad areas *must* team to complement and strengthen each other to make for effective learning experiences for students. Community resources add further dimensions to the instructional team.
5. Teaching teachers *how* to teach with a humanities approach is accomplished easier by having them experience a well taught humanities course themselves — "We usually teach as we were taught."
6. Integrating subject matter requires flexible scheduling, and conditioning to the ringing of bells is soon forgotten.
7. Belief in teachers as educators who can be their own best resource for items and materials if given the opportunity of an open administrative atmosphere.
8. Recognition of the desperate need for more administrative involvement in instructional concerns, such as the need for scheduling instructional team planning periods

together, large blocks of time, and in-service experiences provided for within the school day.

9. No particular approach has been found a panacea. Diversity of program is strongly recommended, with each school selecting its own thrust, according to the decision of the administration, teachers, pupils, and parents working together to decide.

10. The humanities approach offers more avenues for relating to individuals. All teachers and all students can be involved in each day's activities.

For students:

1. A capacity is developed for "enlightened cherishing" of many art forms; appreciation is built in as students are taught with a humanities approach.

2. The individual sees himself at the center of control, able to "ride things" rather than having things ride him.

3. The wide area of the humanities offers the possibility of continuous self-education for an individual.

4. Students discover new interests and see greater potential within selves, hence improving self-image.

5. Chronic absentees in other classes become "turned on" and often have perfect attendance in humanities classes.

6. Students who formerly grew emotional and argumentative in discussions learn to present views calmly and support them intelligently.

7. Students gain confidence and become inspired to create laudable works of art and expressive writing.

8. Students learn to recognize masterpieces of varied art forms and can point out significant characteristics of various artists' styles.

9. Students exhibit initiative to take responsibility for both independent study and group endeavors.

10. Students learn to make critical analyses and to evaluate fairly their own attitudes and actions as well as those of others.

But of all the rewarding returns for students, one recent incident speaks for itself. A little girl who is classified in the counselor's file as below average, apathetic, and dull scrawled her reaction to a humanities course on a scrap of paper thusly:

> This is the best class I have ever had. Every day I can't wait to come in that door because I know something good is going to happen and I know I'm going to be part of it.